BEYOND THE MONEY

"Written by an entrepreneur who's been driven to create massive amounts of success and freedom, *Beyond the Money* will help you achieve the lifestyle shifts you want to keep maximizing yourself, both personally and professionally."
—Dan Sullivan, Cofounder of Strategic Coach, bestselling co-author of *Who Not How* and *The Gap and The Gain*

"Having helped over 100,000 entrepreneurs grow their business and live their ideal life, I can confidently say that Chad has written a masterpiece. This is the book that every successful entrepreneur should read next."
—Gino Wickman, Founder of EOS Worldwide, author of *Traction* and *The EOS Life*

"I work directly with the best of the best all over the world. Chad is changing how the top entrepreneurs live and enjoy their success 'beyond the money.' Highly recommend this book!"
—Nick Nanton, 22-Time Emmy® Award–Winning Director, *WSJ* bestselling author

"In the four years I've known and worked with Chad Willardson, he's revolutionized how I think and act about money and success. I'm far wealthier, freer, and more aligned because of what he's taught me. This new book—*Beyond the Money*—stretches my mind and shows me how I can not only reach eight to nine figures, but more importantly, how I can increase my lifestyle and improve every key area of my life."

—Dr. Benjamin Hardy, bestselling author of
Be Your Future Self Now and co-author of *Who
Not How* and *The Gap and the Gain*

"Chad is fully invested in transforming how ultra-successful entrepreneurs approach life. *Beyond the Money* will change how you think and live once you've made it."

—Gareb Shamus, Founder of Comic Con,
HeroMaker Studios, and Wizard Entertainment

"Even after reaching a high level of financial success, most entrepreneurs struggle to fully own their freedom and maximize their life. *Beyond the Money* shares exactly how we can make those lifestyle shifts. Powerful insights!"

—JJ Virgin, celebrity nutritionist,
four-time *NYT* bestselling author

BEYOND THE MONEY

8 Lifestyle Shifts for Entrepreneurs with 8 Figures or More

CHAD WILLARDSON, CRPC˚, AWMA˚

LIONCREST
PUBLISHING

BEYOND THE MONEY
8 Lifestyle Shifts for Entrepreneurs with 8 Figures or More

ISBN   978-1-5445-3672-9   *Hardcover*
       978-1-5445-3673-6   *Paperback*
       978-1-5445-3674-3   *Ebook*
       978-1-5445-3675-0   *Audiobook*

www.strategiccoach.com

This book is dedicated to each of you who refuses to be held back by the limited imaginations of those around you. Who get excited by the uncertainty and opportunity and inspire others to join you in the journey. To you who are the actual doers of big things, not the talkers. You aim big and refuse to accept the status quo. You have ambitions to change the world and the confidence to go out and do it. Each of you are friends, clients, and mentors who inspire me to reach higher.

CONTENTS

INTRODUCTION

This book is not for everyone. It will never sell a million copies or reach a massive audience.

But that's okay. I didn't write this book for a big audience. I wrote this book for a very small and exclusive group of people. My other books apply to millions of families around the world.

I wrote this book specifically for people like you, and there simply aren't a lot of you around. Reaching your level of success inherently makes you very different from the crowd, so the typical life advice doesn't apply. You're part of a small, elite, and often misunderstood cohort: people who have "made it" financially and are interested to explore what's next.

You've reached this level not because of your endless pursuit of money, but because of your thirst for total freedom. Total freedom means that of lifestyle and time. It does not mean to add more zeros to your bank account or accumulate a never-ending inventory of possessions. You seek growth and success because you value freedom. The freedom to pursue your biggest impact and your real purpose in life. The freedom to move toward your passions and bring others with you. The freedom to dedicate energy and resources to your health and your relationships. The freedom to explore what legacy means to you.

That's what you'll find in this book: how to maximize and optimize your opportunities now that you've come this far. But you won't just hear advice from me. I tapped my network of friends and clients who are some of the top entrepreneurs in the world and people I respect the most. They've been gracious enough to share their insights and experiences in this book.

You might find it odd that, as the owner of a fiduciary wealth management firm, I have not included any investment advice in this book.

(Something else I did on purpose.)

That's because if you're reading this book, you don't need to worry much about money anymore. If you haven't reached a high level of monetary success yet, that's okay too! You might be reading this because you aspire to get there someday. But you need to know that you picked up the wrong title. I encourage you to read *Stress-Free Money* instead and come back to this one once you've achieved total financial independence. Keep climbing.

...Still with me? Good.

Do you ever feel like there are very few people you can relate to given your level of success? Does it sometimes feel lonely at the top? Do you still face business stress and a level of busyness that you should have long delegated to someone else, but you just can't seem to give up that level of control? Is connecting with others harder the more successful you become? Do you find that as soon as you climb one mountain, you're already quickly looking to find your next mountain to climb? Have you neglected your personal health and relationships as you've scaled mountain after mountain? Are you inundated by requests to collaborate, invest, speak, you name it? Are you toying with what retirement might look like for you? Are you wondering how where you've been and where you're going might intersect with your purpose and legacy?

As someone who has personally counseled people like you for twenty years, I can relate to your challenges and anticipate your struggles more than the typical "financial planner." I'm also willing to give you the straightforward advice you need to hear that most people would be afraid to tell you. You're used to being praised and admired everywhere you go, which makes constructive, critical, direct, and informed advice that much more valuable (and rare). I'm not a yes man. People at your level need someone who genuinely understands your situation and isn't afraid to say something when you need to get your act together and make changes. You'll see in this book that I'll tell it like it is.

Most people are intimidated by your success, but I've dealt with people like you for twenty years. I'm not intimidated. You and I are similar in many ways. I'm not here to tell you what you want to hear. I'm here to tell you what you need to hear if you truly want to achieve all the freedoms and fulfillment beyond the money.

Let's get started.

"Connecting with others gives us a sense of inclusion, connection, interaction, safety, and community. Your vibe attracts your tribe, so if you want to attract positive and healthy relationships, be one! Staying connected and getting reconnected feeds the flow of goodness which empowers our humanity."

—SUSAN C. YOUNG

ONE

DON'T BE SUCCESSFUL IN ISOLATION

T hough the world's tallest mountains have fascinated people since the dawn of time, not many people have the ambition to attempt to climb them. If you are the type of person who wants to climb to these mountain peaks, you can't prepare for the feat or get advice from someone on mountaineering the world's tallest peaks from a nonclimber. If you're trying to reach the top, you need to talk with other people high up on that trail, where the air is thinner. There is a big difference between getting advice about your climb from a travel agent versus using a travel guide. Finding travel agents is easy. They're everywhere. But what you really need are travel guides.

If you associate with people who have no desire or interest in summiting, you won't find the resources, ideas, and connections you would if you'd surrounded yourself with like-minded, ambitious climbers. Once you do find those people who have that same high vision as you do, you notice the connection and chemistry right away. Your conversations together bring energy and excitement. You hit it off with them because you can talk about how to get there without being judged for wanting to climb the mountain peaks in the first place.

Once you get to the top and take in the view, it's also much better to have someone to share it with. Hiking to the peak alone is not my cup of tea. For me, it's all about the journey with people I care about. Climbing the mountain alone just for the sake of sticking your flag at the top and saying you did it is less fulfilling—and it's much harder. There's no support or teamwork involved.

TRUSTED CONFIDANTS

One of the biggest challenges entrepreneurs face is feeling like they have no one they can openly talk to. You can't talk to your colleagues and team the same way you can to a fellow founder or CEO. There are very few people with whom you can be totally open and honest with who will understand what you're going through. The more successful you get, the fewer people relate to you.

As you succeed and grow, situations and experiences that seemed extraordinary and out of reach five or ten years ago become very normal to you. Because you live life so differently, you're often a misfit or an outcast in most groups. People look at you differently because frankly, you can afford to do things that they cannot, which sometimes fosters resentment.

Even in Disney movies for small children, the wealthiest character tends to be a villain or a bad guy who acquired their fortune and fame through some corrupt means. From childhood, we see people with money as mean, evil, selfish, or greedy. We're conditioned to see the person who has achieved more and wonder why they think they're so special.

. . .

Successful people often find they have no one to talk to about their challenges and struggles, because people will look at them and say, "Oh, give me a break. Poor you." Of course, the fact is ultrawealthy

*people have their own struggles, self-doubt, mental
health issues, and all the rest, just like everyone else.*

. . .

You don't worry about affording a trip or buying groceries,
but you still go through hard times and difficult life decisions. It's doubly hard to face a challenge in isolation or while
feeling misunderstood, judged, and resented.

Early in her career, Dr. Brandie Keates would field questions
from friends like, "Why do you work all the time?" or "Why
can't you just relax once in a while?" However, she says, "My
businesses are my passions and my dreams. To be mediocre
or to spend your life not trying to make it better than when
you left it seems pointless to me." She needed to find other
friends who would understand and support her ambition,
rather than trying to always keep it in check.

Mike Wandler, President of L&H Industrial, found that before
he increased his education and expanded his professional
network, the people around him often exhibited "crabs in
bucket syndrome...But then I started finding more like-
minded people as my goals and mind expanded."

"As you become more successful, you unintentionally distance
yourself from certain friends/acquaintances who don't share

the growth mindset you have," says Frank Murgic, Founder at Community Care Pharmacy and President at Sunshine Drugs Limited. "You realize they may be holding you back from your true potential."

. . .

If you're reading this book, I'll bet you have ambitious, big goals and you're a natural "visionary." There's a saying that you can't tell your big dreams and visions to small-minded people. They won't accept you for who you are, and they'll resent your ambition and success, even though you aren't out to be better than they are—just to follow your own visionary path.

. . .

LIKE-MINDED PEOPLE

I have friends who have internal business partners who can discuss the ten-thousand-foot vision for the business as well as the everyday challenges, HR issues, finances, clients, and the other intimate details of running the business. I haven't had a business partner since I started Pacific Capital by myself, so I can relate to the need for other sources of support and peer feedback.

Of course, not all business partnerships are beneficial. Some people confide in me that they'd rather not have a partner because their partner has such different goals. One of them wants to grow, and the other doesn't. One is looking to get significant cash flow from their business while their partner wants to reinvest all proceeds toward growth. There are myriad challenges when it comes to business partnerships, often similar to having too many cooks in the kitchen. As a result, many of my clients don't have business partners.

Because I'm a solo owner for my primary business (Pacific Capital), I need to reach out and find people in similar circumstances to have peer-to-peer conversations. Otherwise, it can feel like I'm in a silo. A few years ago, I felt I didn't have anyone to talk to regarding the decisions I was making or to help guide me in achieving big business goals. It's not always appropriate to confide in an employee, and I don't always want to burden my wife—plus, I need someone who has the context of being in the driver's seat of a fast-growing business who can exchange experiences with me, instead of just me offloading concerns and struggles on someone who has never been in my shoes.

To address this issue, in the past few years, I've sought out relationships with growth-focused entrepreneurs who can relate to me. I joined the 10x and Free Zone Strategic Coach programs with Dan Sullivan in Toronto and Chicago, which has helped me meet many ambitious entrepreneurs. I've attended Genius Network conferences in Arizona. These entrepreneurs have achieved very high levels of success, and we can brainstorm together, share ideas, and have conversations we couldn't have anywhere else. The conversations go both ways—we share and learn from each other. It's also highly valuable to have so many different perspectives from so many high achievers across industries.

Successful people I talk to frequently cite Strategic Coach and other entrepreneur mastermind programs for high achievers as instrumental to their business success and to maintaining their sanity. For example, Justin Breen, bestselling author of *Epic Business*, says, "For most of my life, I couldn't find anyone who understood what I was talking about. Only after joining groups like Strategic Coach and Abundance 360 did I meet fellow global entrepreneurs who spoke the same language."

. . .

The byproduct of being an unusually high achiever is not being relatable to most people. They tend to look at you differently, and you command a presence in the room. As a result, I find in my own life, people look to me for leadership, help, and advice, but that street doesn't always go both ways.

They don't want to hear my struggles, or if they're open to it, they can't relate. They wouldn't have empathy because they assume if I'm financially successful, I've got it made. What right do I have to complain? Not being able to have those conversations creates a sense of always being onstage, forever in the spotlight. We all need human connection and outlets for support, though.

...

Dr. Keates could not find the connection and support she needed, so she "sought help, vetting different options to immerse myself in people who have the possibility thinking but also were actually out trying to change the world." The search paid off: "That feeling of not being a 'freak' or 'insanely driven' or 'fiercely passionate about changing the world' has been instrumental in scaling the next level and being the person that I am instead of hiding it or stifling it to not have the reactions I was getting locally."

CREATE YOUR OWN GROUP

Established entrepreneur mastermind programs aren't the only source of community—you can also create your own. In the summer of 2021, I jumped at the opportunity to form a group for highly successful entrepreneurs interested in growth-focused investing and tax efficiency. Members of this group have nine- or ten-figure net worths but still have interest in discussing investment growth strategies and looking at ways to optimize their money. It was important to all of us to create a forum where we could share investment strategies, life hacks, and health hacks with each other. We're focused on the same goals.

These investors have very high net worths but are still in the game to grow. We represent a small, niche type of group in that we want to stay engaged in business rather than simply "throwing in the towel" and living off our wealth. Having this dinner club creates a peer-to-peer environment that we can't find anywhere else.

I advise looking for similar high-level peer groups in your area. If you can't find one, create one. List out the goals of your group and the ground rules for membership. We have formal agendas and agree to come prepared with presentations every single meeting. It's very structured to get the results we want. We plan out our dinner meetings months in advance because everyone has so many obligations and responsibilities related to their different businesses and travel. It's a group that doesn't have extra time, so we stay focused through formally scheduled specific topics, conversations, and presentations. When we get together, we're efficient and maximize the time.

. . .

Ask yourself these questions: What are your specific needs, goals, and interests that a mastermind group could address? What would you enjoy most connecting with others about to fill any gaps in your current peer relationships?

. . .

Our group leader keeps the agenda extremely structured, much more than what I ever would have come up with on my own. Nearly every member of our group has served as a YPO Chair at some point. The benefits of the structure are keeping everyone on track. We create value and a sense of purpose through being prepared. You can't just show up and wing it.

We come ready with specific investment strategies others can implement, for instance, or a health hack that could help the group. It doesn't fly to show up and brag about a big success; you have to come with a strategy that can be implemented by other members in our group. If you share what you've accomplished, you need to be prepared to teach others how to do it too.

There's no fear of giving secrets to the competition because the members of our group think abundantly. We each know that wealth creation and growth is not a zero-sum game. If someone invested in an apartment complex in an up-and-coming tech city, then they can explain how they found the real estate, updated the building, added amenities, and increased rents over time to increase ROI. They'll spell out the steps they took to achieve success and share contact information so other interested investors in our group can pursue it. We don't keep the recipes a secret.

We also bring a challenge we're dealing with and need advice on, whether related to our business, our health, our employees, our finances, or something else. It's valuable because we're all somewhat vulnerable, which is an opportunity we don't have in many settings. We can be honest about our struggles and get suggestions and advice from a high-character group of people we trust. We go around the room and take turns sharing.

PRO TIP

Seek out growth-focused entrepreneurs to whom you can relate. If they have similar ambitions, they probably have similar challenges. First, try professional organizations such as YPO, Strategic Coach, Genius Network, EO, Abundance 360, etc.

If you can't find a group, *create one*. You've been growing people and ideas your whole career. Why should this be any different?

A key component of the model is sharing a highlight idea as well as a struggle we need help with. The struggle conversation often lasts longer than the investment strategy discussion. People want to jump in with helpful advice and guidance that we wouldn't receive anywhere else.

Derek Lobo, CEO of and Broker of Record at SVN Rock Advisors, does something similar.

"I do something called Saturday Mornings with Smart People," he said. "I invite people through every platform available to me to join me for breakfast. I always buy. And it doesn't matter what you do or what industry you're in, you just have to be very smart. I've made a point of hanging out with smart people. I always try to meet with people younger than me and older than me so that I am not living in an echo chamber."

STAY CURIOUS, STAY HUMBLE

In discussing finding like-minded peers, Will Duke, President and CEO of 3Sixty Integrated and who recently sold a company for eight figures, says, "Curiosity is one of the main superpowers for all the top entrepreneurs I have ever met. Curiosity also comes from a place of not thinking you know it all and that there is always more to learn."

I couldn't agree more. Derek and Will are 100 percent correct. Curiosity includes humility—being willing to learn, go out in the world, and see what you don't know. The know-it-alls don't make it far. I've always taught my team in any business that I want them to be learn-it-alls, not know-it-alls. Coachability and humility are traits of successful people and allow them to find each other instead of staying isolated.

Will continues, "When I meet someone that is exceptionally smart, has high self-awareness and...has obviously done a lot of personal and professional development, I ask them who they hang out with, what they read, and what events they go to," allowing him to quickly get a sense of who they are.

. . .

I, too, often ask people what books they're reading. I also get asked, so I keep a log of the books that I'm reading. I can then screenshot or copy and paste this list when people ask for recommendations without needing to reinvent the answer every time. These conversations help identify which groups a person is a part of, what influences they allow into their life to help them grow, and whether you would want them as an influence in your own life.

. . .

Make sure you're surrounding yourself with people who approach life with great energy and enthusiasm. These types of connections will keep your spirits up as you break new trails, not complainers and victim-minded people who will sap your energy. There will be times on the journey when one of you absolutely wants to sit down and give up. However, if you have other ambitious people around you who want to achieve great milestones with you, you can keep each other going.

KEY TAKEAWAYS

- The byproduct of being an unusually high achiever is not being "relatable" to many people.

- At this level, you don't worry about affording a trip or buying groceries, but you still go through hard times and difficult decisions. It's doubly hard to face a challenge in isolation or while feeling misunderstood, judged, and resented.

- Look for groups or professional organizations that attract other like-minded peers with whom you can connect.

- Your net worth isn't the only thing that should continue to grow. If you can't find a group with other like minds to facilitate that growth, use your skill as a visionary and create one.

"Celebrating your wins not only feels great physically, it also reinforces the positive attitude and behavior you want to have show up when you face a new challenge or opportunity."

—BILL CARMODY

TWO

GIVE YOURSELF PERMISSION TO CELEBRATE

To many high-achieving, growth-minded people, pausing to celebrate feels like a waste of time. It seems unproductive. They're already on to the next achievement and the next mountain to climb. They don't stop and sit at the top to celebrate or reflect on the mountain they just climbed; instead, they instantly look around for the next summit. Stopping and celebrating is not what got them there, and they don't want to lose ground. They have a constant need for high achievement. It can be a real struggle to pause and relax.

Does this sound like you?

Celebration may not naturally be in your DNA. Whether you were born a high achiever or learned your approach to life through your environment, I'll bet you feel a constant urgency to keep growing and achieving. Growth is great, but don't miss out on recognizing and celebrating with your co-achievers, whether your spouse, family, team members, or clients. "Celebrating a win gives you a chance to thank people who helped plus give yourself an increased sense of positivity and gratitude," Tim Thackrah, startup investor, coach, and mentor, notes.

SHARE THE MOMENT

It's extremely important to take the time to recognize the achievement with everyone who has been on the journey with you. People who are about to sell their business often ask me what to do. I always say the first thing you should do is absolutely nothing. The next thing you should do is take your spouse or partner out and celebrate the moment, because it took a great deal of hard work to reach where you are. Then take the time to write down your reflections on the journey.

Writing down your reflections, lessons, and experiences is valuable because it memorializes the achievement. There's benefit to getting ideas out of your head and onto paper—by hand, with a pen. That act clarifies your thinking and makes it more material. It's critical to take the opportunity to reflect on where you started, what's changed, the challenges you overcame, and lessons you've learned along the way. In Dr. Benjamin Hardy and Dan Sullivan's book *The Gap and The Gain*, they write, "The way to measure your progress is backward against where you started, not against your ideal." If you're engaging in this reflection, think about how what you've just accomplished relates to your purpose.

What are the greatest lessons you've learned in getting to this point?

A client recently sold his national business, and after hearing my advice, he got a sitter for his kids for the weekend and took his wife on a trip to celebrate. They talked about the struggles they endured to reach their success and how their life was changing as a result of the sale. They wrote down their hopes for the future for their family and their little kids. He was grateful to take a step back to reflect instead of getting right back on the hamster wheel for his next venture.

One of our top clients sold his business in a major transaction worth nearly a billion dollars, and he actually gave million-dollar bonuses to some of his key people who'd been there for over twenty years. He was extremely excited to be making their families millionaires because of the massive business deal he created. He was able to celebrate not just with his family but to create celebrations in each of their families too.

PRO TIP

Write down not only what you have to celebrate, but the challenges you overcame along the way. You can share this with a loved one or keep it to yourself; the important part is that you *make time to do it*. Having a practice of gratitude every day, even if it's only five minutes, can truly change your life.

Celebration isn't limited to big wins either. "I celebrate wins all the time," Justin Breen, Founder and CEO of BrEpic Communications LLC, says, "from buying my wife flowers when signing with a new partner, to throwing launch parties and other events for my companies." He also writes a grateful journal post every weekday on LinkedIn. "When you're constantly grateful and celebrating wins, it's hard to be ungrateful or unhappy."

Mike Wandler agrees. He and his team devote time to "talking about or listing my wins, counting my blessings, looking at the positives...that's the key to happiness: before you focus on what's wrong or what you want to improve, list all the things that are going right."

THE JOURNEY VERSUS
THE DESTINATION

Justin Dalton, CEO of Dalton Enterprises, says:

> Once we achieve "wins" it's so tempting to just move on to the next challenge and keep grinding away, which defeats the purpose of reflecting on and growing from the experience you've just been through. It really has always been more about the journey than the destination for me, which has been fulfilling in its own right but leaves the destination a bit more hollow as a result. I think it's critical for entrepreneurs to start with the end in mind so that they can celebrate and enjoy the destination more when they finally arrive.

He's had experience in selling a large family businesses and having big success windfalls, so he speaks from great experience. He likes building, creating, and overcoming challenges, which is true of most clients I work with. It tends to be anti-climactic when they finally sell their business and get all the money. When looking back, there is often more enjoyment in the pursuit and the journey than in the destination.

They've prepared for the hundred-mile ultramarathon, enjoying the training and who they've mentally and physically had to become to get to that big event. Finishing the race puts a nice stamp on the work, but it isn't the real reward. The nine months of training to become good enough to complete the goal were the reward.

I've watched friends complete those races, and finishing is almost a letdown. It's common for them to go to a confused or dark place mentally, because they lose a clarifying purpose. After meeting a big long-term goal, your identity can feel up in the air. You might find yourself looking around, feeling exposed, and wondering, *Now what? What am I working toward now that I finished that?*

· · ·

If you meet your goal and have nothing else to train for or look forward to, you'll lose all the fitness you gained. It's important to continually find new ways and whys to maintain your drive.

· · ·

MEASURE THE GAIN

High-achieving people will never stop cold turkey. You don't hit one home run and then stop playing a game. You keep swinging. It's not in your DNA (and is probably bad for your health) to go from full speed to a complete stop. That attribute got you where you are, but it's still important to pause, celebrate, and recognize.

The Gap and the Gain, written by my client and friends Dr. Benjamin Hardy and Dan Sullivan, is a life changer. I recommend it to every teenager, every adult...everyone.

Chad Johnson, CEO, entrepreneur, author, husband, and father of eleven, has been following the book's guidance for seventeen years and "can't imagine" his life without it. "I win every day, every week, every month, and every year! No joke!" He says the approach has been a "life changer" and "has completely rewired my brain and transformed my happiness in life. Prior to that awareness I was never satisfied and always striving. Not a great way to live abundantly. Now I get to live in the gain!"

The book's approach cultivates gratitude, excitement, and positivity by changing the way you measure results. The authors argue happiness depends on how you measure your life. If you're looking at an ideal future you haven't yet reached, then you'll always fall short. The ideal future is a mirage. You'll never reach it.

Say you're trying to lose thirty pounds and have lost fifteen. You're not at your ideal weight yet. Looking at a picture in a magazine of some buff model who's thinner than you will only highlight the gap between the you today versus the "ideal" you. Constantly measuring against that ideal is not only unrealistic but will also perpetuate unhappiness. Focusing on the gap of falling short leads to unhappiness.

By contrast, Dr. Hardy and Dan Sullivan explain that the gain means measuring your progress backward. When you measure backward, you can see and celebrate that you've lost fifteen pounds. Looking at the old you compared to the current you reveals you've made great gains and progress, which feels good. That good feeling then helps push you forward to make more progress.

. . .

The whole notion of celebrating progress, focusing on positives, and practicing gratitude stems from measuring backward rather than forward. Measuring forward, you'll always be in the gap and unhappy about falling short. By contrast, if you measure looking for progress backward, you can see the gains and feel happiness.

. . .

If you focus on your child's one B+ and why they didn't get straight A's, you'll highlight the negative and downplay their success. On the other hand, if you ask how they got all the A's they did earn, you'll celebrate and promote their continued success. The difference comes from choosing to measure the gain rather than the gap, and it's a hugely powerful mindset.

KEEP CLIMBING UPWARD

It's possible to live in the gain and still keep climbing. Your continuous ambition is part of who you are. "Never feeling satisfied is both a blessing and a burden," according to Vess Pearson, CEO of Aptive Environmental. "However, it does drive you and pushes you to grow. I've accepted it is who I am. It's both positive and negative."

Craig Coppola started his company, Lee & Associates Arizona, in 1991 and reports that he still works in and on it to this day. "The mountains are there in the business but also in life," he says. "Keeping a marriage happy and growing. Raising four kids. Growing as a person." There are "lots of mountains," he says, and "all goals don't all have to be about business."

You can find ways to celebrate as you go. Dr. Keates, owner of many chiropractic clinics in the Northeast, says, "I get more satisfaction or celebration in being one-on-one with a patient or a team member and knowing that I truly understand them" and "helped them unlock something to improve their life...leav[ing] them in a better place than when I first encountered them."

Celebrate with someone. The journey is better with others.

KEY TAKEAWAYS

- It's not in your DNA (and is probably bad for your health) to go from full speed to a complete stop when it comes to continued achievements. That attribute got you where you are, but it's still important to pause, recognize, and celebrate your wins.

- Whom you celebrate with matters. It's extremely important to take the time to recognize the achievement with everyone who has been on the journey with you.

- Celebration doesn't have to be limited to big windfalls. Cultivate more positivity in your life by changing the way you measure results. When you see more wins and are constantly celebrating, you're practicing gratitude that can greatly improve your attitude and motivation.

- Write down your reflections on the win to help solidify them in your mind and to build celebration consistency.

"Things that matter most
must never be at the mercy of
things that matter least."

—JOHANN WOLFGANG VON GOETHE

THREE

RECHARGE YOUR RELATIONSHIPS

N ow that you're at the mountaintop financially and have a clearer picture of the horizon, you can use that view to see what others in your life struggle with. If you received help along your journey, then you can pay that good fortune forward by assisting others in reaching the summit, personally or professionally. Look around—who else needs you? In thinking about how to conduct myself, I remember this advice: don't take the elevator to the top without sending it back down.

. . .

You've worked harder than the average person and are more driven than the average person, which is a positive—but don't make the mistake of communicating to people that your work and your money is more important than your family and your relationships.

. . .

Reaching great success in your business requires laser focus, which can lead to relationships receiving less time and attention than they deserve. Once you've achieved financial independence, it's time to recharge your relationships.

I'll be blunt: most people in your life—including your significant other, your children, and your close personal friends—don't understand you. They don't share your ambition. You're built differently; it's just a fact. They don't understand how you're still motivated and focused on growth. Trying to explain to them what's going on inside you is difficult, because they can't relate to it. Instead of trying to justify where you've been and what's driven you to get where you are, focus on recharging connections with the people who matter most.

. . .

Learn to put the same focus, attention, and investment into your relationships as you have into your business. Investing in your relationships pays dividends and yields a long-term ROI. To recharge your relationships and ensure the people most important to you get prioritized, you need a mission statement. You need specific goals for your relationships. Look at them with the same care, focus, and weighty importance as you've looked at clients, associates, financial statements, and business goals.

. . .

As with investing, it's very difficult to make up for lost time. You need to start investing in relationships with the people you care about right away. That's one commitment I made before my business career even started. My wife and I got married as young college students back in 2001. I saw fellow students take jobs with prestigious brand names that were going to require three to five years of corporate slavery. Family time and relationships were not things I was willing to ignore for years at a time just to impress a boss or get a promotion. I never worked hundred-hour weeks for the big corporation because it wasn't worth it to me. But I know most highly successful people have made decisions to sacrifice relationships in pursuit of money, at least for a certain period of their life.

. . .

True wealth is in your relationships,
not your riches.

. . .

Where you invest now will impact what you have in twenty years. What would bring you the most fulfillment in the next decade or two? Where should your time, energy, and attention go? When you're on your deathbed, I'm sure you won't say you wish you'd spent more time at the office or on your computer playing email ping-pong.

SCHEDULE IT

It's time to get your loved ones on your calendar. Preschedule distraction-free relationship-building time with the people you care about. If you put it on your calendar in advance, you'll be there. I had to learn that what isn't on my calendar doesn't happen. My friends or business colleagues and I used to play phone tag, so I started scheduling nearly all of my calls through my executive assistant so we could set aside time on my Google calendar.

I've also made an "ideal weekly calendar" for my EA, with each day's purpose identified, what I'd like to focus on for the day and who I'd ideally spend my time with. Now, my EA schedules time-blocked activities for both work and my personal life. I have time on my calendar for my wife and kids, or doing things like taking my mom out to lunch for her birthday. We don't miss important events because we are very intentional with what makes it on the calendar.

PRO TIP

Sit down and look at the next three months on your calendar. Schedule time to spend with your loved ones each week, distraction-free. If you have multiple children, include some one-on-one activities with each of them too.

If it's on the calendar, it's nonnegotiable and cannot be moved for work. Communicate this to your team. Once you see the impact this small change can make in your relationships, you won't turn back to the old way of doing things.

If you want to go on dates with your spouse or significant other, you'd better make time for it, or it won't happen. I pre-schedule dates, give my EA ideas of places to book so we have the time blocked out and the reservation in place in advance.

Now, my wife and I can look at the calendar to see what we're doing in the coming week and know we have that time blocked off. My EA also schedules our trips and uses a travel app called TripIt. This way, the three of us can see all upcoming travel, business and personal. It's easier to focus on work and business activities knowing we have some fun dates or trips already planned ahead of time. We have something to look forward to that nurtures our relationship. My wife can see I've prioritized our relationship because it's already on the calendar.

. . .

If you are very organized in your business scheduling but you decide to just "wing it" for your personal life and family, then other reasons, excuses, and distractions will crop up and seem important in the moment but divert you from your relationship goals. Calendaring keeps you on track and holds you accountable to actually prioritize what you say is a priority.

. . .

You know how to make happen what you schedule for your business. If you book time with your most important clients and business partners, you don't miss those meetings. Yet somehow, high achievers back out on their kids, best friends, or spouse when they should keep those dates in just as high, if not higher, regard. If you've made those trade-offs in the past, it's time to recharge your relationships by putting them on your calendar.

TIGHTEN YOUR INNER CIRCLE

Focus on your personal inner circle, the people you care about most. Maybe you work with some of them, but this time isn't about doing business. The goal is to revive personal relationships that haven't received the investment they deserve.

Maybe, like me, you haven't had to sacrifice and abandon time with the people you care about. If you're already good at devoting time to your relationships, great. Now that you have financial abundance, you can give even more to the relationships in your life. You have financial freedom and even more time and opportunities to make an impact. Use your expertise to mentor and help them with whatever they're struggling with. Maybe there are friends you lost touch with and want to return to.

I know someone whose mom was suddenly diagnosed with terminal cancer. By reprioritizing their relationships and schedules, they were able to take time to make a big impact for their mom before she passed. In my own life, I've been spending more time trying to help my mom. She's young, active, and healthy, but a couple of years ago, she received a diagnosis of a rare form of Parkinson's disease. I block out time every day to call my mom and strive to spend time with her as often as possible. I even took her as my guest to an industry conference in Kauai (my wife graciously gave up her spot), and that time alone together was precious. I also have made time to utilize my connections and network to access potential medical specialists to help my mom's situation.

If you've missed your kids' awards assemblies or sports practices and games, now's the time to recharge those relationships as quickly as possible. You can't make up for lost time, but you can start being better today. Or if you've participated in the past but were distracted by your business concerns, now you can invest your attention in being more fully present. If you're constantly checking your emails or staring at your phone during your family time, that's a clue that things need to change. You're successful enough to have someone else monitor the minute-to-minute needs of your businesses and investments. My friends Jim and Jamie Sheils wrote the book *The Family Board Meeting* and created the accompanying website, 18Summers.com. They offer parents ideas for monthly or quarterly one-on-one, four-hour activities to do with their kids—with no phones. My kids and I have created special memories using the concepts and ideas they teach.

Dr. Brandie Keates, the founder and CEO of Experience Chiropractic and Bloom, says now that money is not her main focus, "The relationship I have with myself outside of my identity at work as well as my relationship with my children and my family is my top priority."

I know as well as anyone how tremendously hard it is to build a truly successful business. You've done a great job juggling so many competing concerns and addressing demands to get where you are today. Now you can enjoy the fruits of your labor, including having more time, and you can share that abundance with the people you care about. Boost your investment of time and energy into your relationships. You can't manufacture human connection; you must nurture it over the long haul. It requires both quality *and* quantity of time together. Time and relationships are our most precious assets and need to be cherished as such.

Getting to the top of the mountain may have meant leaving some people you care about back at base camp for a while. Now that you've succeeded financially, you have no excuse to neglect the people you love. Recharge your relationship with them and share what you've learned on your adventures. You have more freedom with your time. Use it wisely.

KEY TAKEAWAYS

- Reaching great success in your business requires laser focus, which can lead to relationships receiving less time and attention than they deserve.

- As with investing, it's very difficult to make up for lost time. You need to start investing in relationships with the people you care about right away.

- Preschedule distraction-free relationship-building time with the people you care about. If you put it on your calendar in advance, you'll be there.

- If you're constantly checking your emails or staring at your phone during your family time, that's a clue that things need to change. You're successful enough to have someone else monitor the minute-to-minute needs of your businesses and investments.

"Your health and well-being should be your number one priority, nothing else is more important."

—ROBERT CHEEKE

FOUR

PRIORITIZE AND INVEST IN YOUR HEALTH

To climb a mountain, you need to come prepared with hydration and nutrition, in addition to training and getting physically fit. You can't show up weak, hungry, and unrested at the foot of Mt. Everest and expect to make it to the top alive—let alone survive the descent and celebrate your accomplishment. Even so, it's far too common for high achievers to neglect their personal health.

People in high-responsibility positions have higher stress and higher rates of heart attack and other health complications.

Positions of leadership and power can lead to high-stress and imbalanced lives. People often think they can worry about their health later and focus on their business and career now, but you can't put off your health. You'll pay much more down the road, if you make it that far.

. . .

Extremely busy, active entrepreneurs are motivated by achievement, success, connection, and financial rewards. Health often doesn't necessarily check any of those boxes, so it gets put on hold. Some people I know are so busy that they make no time at all for their health, even though their body is the engine that drives all their success and achievement. Taking care of the engine is nonnegotiable.

. . .

High-achieving people have many demands on their time and sometimes think there are more pressing issues than health at the moment, but it doesn't work to put your body on the back burner. It's a challenge to find the energy to keep up with your schedule, so you often over-caffeinate just to stay in the game.

My health-focused clients ultimately get so much more done. They take good care of themselves and have a higher quality of life for longer. In contrast, the others are always uptight, tightly wound, and stressed out. They don't exercise as much as they should. They don't eat healthy (always eating on the run), they travel like crazy for work, and they are completely overscheduled. They're in a constant loop of artificial stimulants to keep themselves afloat, because otherwise they'd crash and burn.

. . .

Don't wait for illness to start prioritizing wellness.

. . .

"The older I get, the more this topic is so critical because the health of an organization is directly linked to the health of its leadership," Dr. Keates says. "In the end, when you have success and everything that you desire," you cannot enjoy it "if you do not have your health."

MIND AND BODY

Mental and physical health go hand in hand. Running a business represents a great deal of stress, and stress is the number one cause of disease. Highly successful people feel like they're always onstage. People expect them to have all the right answers. They lead others, make the hard decisions, and deal with the biggest problems. The serious issues in an organization come to them. They can't completely escape that burden.

Most working people can disappear at 5:00 p.m. and take a break from the job responsibilities on their plate, but you're not like most people. Entrepreneurs don't clock out at 5:00 p.m. There's no point when they can fully stop thinking about the business. Successful entrepreneurs go 24/7, both by nature and job description. Those demands take a significant toll on the body and on the mind.

If you don't take care of the machine—the body and your mental and physical health—you'll burn out. Burnout and stress-induced health issues represent a major challenge. Many people depend on you. You're carrying the burdens of one or more businesses, investments, partnerships, multiple people and their families, many clients and customers. Without taking care of yourself, you'll collapse.

"Health is more than just physical," Frank Murgic says. "It is also spiritual, mental, and emotional. Being in top health allows me to be the best me. I want to be able to share in the experiences of my children as they grow...to me, health is wealth."

· · ·

Burnout and mental health are major issues among high achievers. When I started my career twenty years ago, I learned suicides are five times higher in my industry than others because of the volatility of the markets and the economy. We constantly experience the stress of major uncertainty and factors outside our control. It's an extremely taxing burden to carry in our industry.

. . .

Ninad Tipnis, Founder and Principal Architect of Mumbai-based JTCPL Designs, said, "Health is one of the most underrated pillars of wealth, even with a lot of financially free people. I have observed that people give far more importance to designing their careers and finances than they give to designing a healthy life. What is the use of all your wealth if you do not have the health to enjoy it?"

I agree completely. Some of my entrepreneurial clients manage that stress by going to silent retreats. For days at a time, they enjoy nature and literally say nothing to anyone. Other ways to deal with stress include exercise, massages, journaling, meditation, getting out in nature, enjoying fresh air, supplementing with vitamin D, connecting with peers, unplugging from technology, and opening up and sharing your struggles. All these behaviors can benefit both mental and physical health.

It's absolutely critical to invest in your physical and mental health. You cannot neglect them and expect to be successful in other areas of your life. You will eventually burn out and crumble and may incur long-term consequences.

Failing to manage your mental health can undermine your financial and marital goals. Disagreements about money are a leading cause of divorce and a major source of stress. Stress is the number one cause of disease. These are major factors in your quality of life, which is why I wrote my first book, *Stress-Free Money*.

INVEST IN YOUR HEALTH

There's a saying: "A healthy person has a thousand wishes, a sick person only one."

Longevity and health span require making sacrifices now so that you don't have to make the major sacrifices later, just like financial investing. If you put in the consistent effort now, then in twenty-five years, you'll reap the compound effects of your choices. Consistency produces massive financial rewards and results as well as health rewards and results. "Health is not something that can be purchased, and just like anything of value, it needs maintenance," Dr. Keates says.

When you're sixty-five, you can't go back and make up for thirty years of missed investment opportunities. That time is gone. It's done. The same goes for health. You are where you are and can't go back. You can mitigate your situation, but you can't fully make up for neglecting your health. So truly good health takes consistent discipline and intentional effort to stay on track.

PRO TIP

Hire a highly recommended personal trainer, nutrition coach and/or a mental health professional to guide you on your health journey. Not only will you see the results of your efforts more quickly, but you will also be more inclined to keep this commitment to yourself if it's scheduled in advance and you're paying someone who is a qualified expert.

Where personal health and longevity falls in your life depends on your exact priorities. Chad Johnson, for instance, has pioneered a system called Giant Five™, ranking priorities in order of faith, marriage, children, health, and using God-given talents. The important part is health must make the list of top priorities—and then you must act on it, with diligence and regularity, because the results compound over time.

Devoting time to health doesn't take away from your success; quite the contrary. When I'm more health focused, I reap the benefits in my business. Dan Sullivan says as a high-achieving entrepreneur, the two things you have to protect the most are your confidence and your energy. That advice has stuck with me ever since I became a client of Strategic Coach. My fitness decisions markedly impact my confidence and my energy, rippling out to every aspect of my personal, professional, and financial success.

When I start my morning with very intentional exercise and hydration after sleeping well and eating well, I see the results in my performance. When I avoid processed junk foods and treat my body better, my day is noticeably better and my energy stays high. I can get more done in my business. Successful entrepreneurs not only understand this relationship but actually make it a core discipline in their life.

"Being healthy and having a strong immune system brings a great sense of confidence," Mark Choe, entrepreneur and Co-owner of the Pines Resort, says. "I have the feeling that I have a lot of time to achieve very big dreams."

Health has always been on my mind, but I've had different commitment levels throughout my journey. Lately I've become much more committed after learning how much quality and quantity of sleep impact health. I've taken these past couple years to really study health, personal care, wellness, exercise, and fitness. As a result, I pay more attention to my health than I used to. Three recent "investments" I made have given a great boost to our family's personal health and overall well-being. I hired a personal chef, a fitness trainer/nutrition coach, and a personal massage therapist. They make such a positive difference in our lives that my wife and I could not imagine how we managed without them. I also joined a new program called "Lifetime Extender" offered by Dan Sullivan and Strategic Coach. Many leading health experts are coming together in this group to provide cutting-edge research and resources on the topic of living healthier and longer, making it possible for the age of your body to be much lower than your chronological age. For instance, you may be sixty but have the physical health of a forty-five-year-old.

Hal Elrod's book *The Miracle Morning* talks about the powerful morning routines that can set your day up for success. How you start your morning directs the entire day. Prioritizing quality sleep, health, hydration, and exercise will pay dividends in all areas of your life—your relationships, your business, your finances. It's rare to see ultrafinancially successful people with poor health habits, which can't be a coincidence. There's a correlation between your discipline and intention in personal health and your discipline and health in finances and business.

SET YOUR PRIORITIES

"Schedule exercise on your calendar, and don't move it," Vess Pearson advises. "Make it a priority. There's rarely a reason why a meeting needs to be scheduled over your workout."

Tim Thackrah advises getting a personal trainer and says his trainer "is an important part of my team. They have made a massive positive contribution to my ongoing success."

There are many different ways to incorporate good health into a highly productive life, and you'll find your productivity and enjoyment increase the healthier you are. Unhealthy people don't maximize their energy and potential, and in the end, those choices keep them from climbing as many mountains as they'd like.

To that point, Frédéric Brunner, CEO and Co-founder of Genioo, sums up the relationship between health and pursuing your purpose: "I love life, and I love to create things. Personal health is a proxy to be able to create longer and to feel better at all levels."

I agree. Be careful not to neglect your health, so you can focus on continuing on to the next peak.

KEY TAKEAWAYS

- As a high achiever, you have many demands on your time and may sometimes think there are more pressing issues than your health at the moment, but it doesn't work to put your body on the back burner.

- If you don't take care of the machine—your body and your mental and physical health—you'll burn out. Burning out will not only hurt you, but it will hurt everyone who depends on you in your business and, more importantly, in your personal life.

- Longevity and health span require making sacrifices now so that you don't have to make the major sacrifices later, just like financial investing. If you put in the consistent effort now, then in twenty-five years, you'll reap the compound effects of your choices.

- Just like you calendar time to connect with others and celebrate (or, I encourage you to after reading this book), calendar the time you need to take care of yourself. Stick to it like you keep the rest of your commitments.

"Attention is now our most valuable commodity. To live the lives we really want to live, what we actually need to master is managing our attention."

—MAURA THOMAS

FIVE

MANAGE
YOUR
ATTENTION

igh achievers are optimistic about new opportunities. If you're reading this book, I'll bet you love a new challenge, a new opportunity, a new collaboration, a new business idea. It's exciting to get involved with new passion projects, business ideas, collaborative partnerships, speaking engagements, podcasts, interviews, investments, and potential clients. The opportunities are nearly endless, so the demands on our attention are unbelievably high. We get bombarded with emails, texts, and calls vying for our attention. It's nonstop.

. . .

Saying yes to too much can lead to real problems, though. Overwhelm leads to burnout, which, as we've seen, brings stress and damages your health. If you're busy but not productive, you'll become drained of energy.

. . .

It can be hard to know what to say yes to and what to decline when you're so highly skilled and sought after. It's tempting to overcommit your time to opportunities that don't actually warrant your attention. Choosing where to devote your attention is a challenge when all the opportunities have upside potential, so you need a filter and process in place to make those decisions.

Attention management is the practice of controlling distractions, being present in the moment, finding flow, and maximizing focus so that you can unleash your genius. It's about being intentional instead of reactive. We all have the same limited number of hours in the day. You have many priorities, and they're competing for your time and attention (and money). The problem isn't sorting good from bad options; it's choosing which good options to pursue and which good options to turn down. Most choices aren't cut and dried.

THE VALUE OF SETTING FILTERS

You have more investment opportunities than you could possibly pursue, and by the same token, you have more demands and requests for involvement than are humanly possible to say yes to. You must set up filters and boundaries that maximize your strengths and values.

As someone who many people look to as a mentor and thought leader, you might feel pressure to overcommit to "give back," not wanting to let others down. You remember when you were struggling early on and how much you could have benefited from someone with more success and experience, but you can't be that helper to everyone and overcommit yourself. "I have had to say no to mentoring outside my teams and partners," Craig Coppola says. "This is a big lesson and is constantly tested as I want to help and add value but simply cannot do this for everyone."

Managing my attention has always been a challenge. I still haven't perfected it, but I've made major strides in the last three years. I've become more intentional about what gets my attention and what I can have other people pay attention to for me.

Once you know what truly matters to you, you can decide how to prioritize and what gets through your attention filters. I personally plan my days of the week to match certain activities and focuses now. I have a schedule that outlines my ideal week, including who is involved, what activities are happening, and what I will do and not do. My wife knows that ideal week plan. My executive assistant knows it. My entire team at work knows it. There is more of a cadence and rhythm to my week because we have a game plan for each day and what that day entails.

PRO TIP

Sit down and sketch out your ideal work week. Be overly focused and detailed. Designate certain days or times of day for certain activities. Give this schedule to your team and instruct them not to deviate from it. If someone wants to reach you badly enough, they can wait until you've allotted time for that conversation.

Under no circumstances should you be responding to every real-time phone call, text, notification, and email that comes your way. That ends today.

If someone tries to schedule an activity on a day that doesn't match that day's purpose, it's not happening. I now have very clear boundaries and don't allow other obligations to bleed into the prescheduled attention-getters already on my calendar. Mark Choe uses a similar system, saying, "Spending time creating and checking your top priorities quarterly and then daily really helps."

As Vess Pearson puts it, "You have to know your personal virtues. Once those are determined, only pursue opportunities that align entirely with your virtues. Be one hundred percent loyal to your virtues and zero percent to what people think."

. . .

Attention management is our most important defense against a world that is constantly conspiring to steal it.

. . .

Mark Choe agrees: "I definitely still struggle with saying NO to good opportunities as I am such a curious person and always want to do the most, but I have definitely gotten better with age. I always refer back to Derek Siver's 'If it's not a hell yes, than it's a no.'" Mike Wandler adds, "I check in with my head, heart, and gut; if all three say yes, it's a go, full steam ahead. If two say no, I'm out."

In my attention-management system, I know which days will focus on what purpose. For example, a podcast host with a large audience recently reached out to my team to invite me on as a guest for his show. He said for the next couple months, he only has availability on Fridays or Saturdays. While it may have been tempting to my former self to make an exception, we don't compromise the cadence anymore. My executive assistant let the host know that I do podcast interviews on Tuesdays or Wednesdays, so we'd have to find a time later in the year. You can't go to a doctor and say you want surgery on a Sunday morning. There are preset surgery days. The same should be true of your schedule. Name your intentions and take back control of your days.

. . .

Pure hustle and saying yes to a ton of opportunities has gotten people where they are, but at a certain point, that behavior is no longer sustainable. You can't get to the next level unless you switch it up completely and start doing less. If you continually stack more on your plate, you'll burn out. It sounds counterintuitive, but to go big, you have to do less.

. . .

The least successful and most overwhelmed people I know are overly committed, stressed, disheveled, chasing too many rabbits at once, saying yes to everything, and always available. You see them everywhere. The most successful and confident people are focused and intentional. They have time to think and ponder decisions. They don't split their attention in a thousand directions. They don't waste their time and aren't easily distracted. You don't see them everywhere. Subtract commitments and simplify. Increase the quality of what you do while decreasing the quantity. As Derek Sivers points out, "More people die from eating too much than from eating too little."

INVEST YOUR ATTENTION WISELY

Too often, people let others dictate their attention, and attention pays. Why do companies spend $50 million for twenty seconds on a Super Bowl commercial? Because your attention is extremely valuable. If you take complete control of your attention, then you take your life back into your own hands.

. . .

How you use your twenty-four hours a day really is about quality, not quantity. Warren Buffett suggests politely saying no to 95 percent of opportunities. You can't say yes to everything. Where your attention goes, your energy flows—so choose wisely.

. . .

"I say yes to experiences in life with my family and growing networks on a global level," Justin Breen says. "Both of my companies revolve around those two facets. Everything else is a *no*."

You've achieved a level of success by understanding the value of tangible assets and financial investments. Once you've reached a significant level of wealth, attention becomes your most valuable asset as well as your asset most in demand. It's not your time that matters per se but your attention in that time.

The solution? Stop multitasking—focus on only one thing at a time.

You could be physically present in a meeting but paying attention to something else, scrolling on your phone and looking at your texts, emails, notifications, and social media. The world has a constant onslaught of disruptions. The battle for your attention is intense.

"Attention management offers the ability to consciously direct your attention in any given moment, to be more proactive than reactive, and to maintain control rather than inadvertently relinquish it. It's about regaining control over your attention and thereby taking control of your life. Attention management empowers your productivity," Maura Thomas, author of *Attention Management*, says.

As I've implemented a more conscious attention-management system, my primary business has tripled in the last three years. Using my attention on the highest-impact activities has increased our business growth significantly. I am doing less yet accomplishing more. If I'd been bogged down, giving attention to tasks and decisions where I wasn't needed, then we wouldn't have seen that growth. This also takes recognizing that there are many other experts and specialists on your team who would succeed by giving their attention to those things that aren't the highest and best use of your time.

DO NOT DISTURB

Managing my attention and maintaining personal boundaries have helped me have better conversations and relationships with my children and my wife. When I get home from work, I plug in my phone upstairs and then go downstairs to spend time with my family. My attention is on them. I go on one-on-one activity outings with my kids each month, with no phone use. The only approved role for a phone is to take pictures at the event.

My daughter Bentley and I recently went to dinner and a Lakers basketball game in Los Angeles. She's eight years old. I told her I'd only have my phone to take pictures, and otherwise I wouldn't look at it at all. I told her we would talk to each other, and she could ask any questions she wanted. She asked me what it was like when I was eight years old. What was I scared of, and what did I want to be when I grew up? What were my favorite things to learn about in school? Did I always love playing basketball? It was a conversation I will never forget. We bonded as we shared our thoughts about her current stage of life. If my attention was instead on my texts and emails, then I would've missed that special conversation and the moments of connection with her.

Even in smaller increments, you can set aside time with your phone on "do not disturb." Go on a walk with your spouse or child, and don't take your phone with you. Regardless of the demands on your time, you can implement focused attention on the people you care about.

PUT TECHNOLOGY IN ITS PLACE

Technology is incredible and has advanced our society in ways that are too numerous to mention, but it can also present a downside if we rely on it so much that we lose our ability to communicate with people IRL ("in real life").

"Internet addiction has some behavioral similarities to hard drug use," says Antoine Bechara, psychology professor and neuroscientist at the USC Dornsife College of Letters, Arts and Sciences. "The similarities between internet and cocaine addiction really lie in those brain systems that drive you toward the reward."

One of the most important ways to manage your attention is to set time boundaries around phone use. Power off your phone when it's outside of the designated time. Addiction expert Steve Sussman, professor of preventive medicine, psychology, and social work, studies the phenomenon. "Consequences associated with smartphone addiction include lack of concentration and decreased performance at school or work; car and other accidents; possible blurred vision; sleep disturbance and financial costs," Sussman says.

If your phone is constantly sending you push notifications from different apps, you are susceptible to incessant interruptions. I personally have zero notifications enabled, so there are no incoming alerts to disrupt my focus. If it's a designated time to check LinkedIn, missed calls, or texts, then it's on me to unlock my phone and open those apps—I'm not at the mercy of someone sending constant alerts to hijack my attention.

Multitasking is impossible anyway. Multitasking simply means doing two things poorly at the same time. Single-tasking is the only way to get anything done well. There's a real cost to our brains when we continually switch our attention back and forth between tasks. We switch quickly between two things, but get slower results. An article published in *Harvard Business Review* noted that "based on over a half-century of cognitive science and more recent studies on multitasking, we know that multitaskers do less and miss information. It takes time (an average of 15 minutes) to reorient to a primary task after a distraction such as an email. Efficiency can drop by as much as 40%. Long-term memory suffers and creativity—a skill associated with keeping in mind multiple, less common, associations—is reduced."[1]

Everyone is susceptible to this dynamic, but it's even more pressing for entrepreneurs. As the owner of a company, you could have notifications going off every two minutes. A distracted entrepreneur is an unsuccessful entrepreneur. A distracted father is an unsuccessful father. A distracted spouse is an unsuccessful spouse. These issues affect everyone. If you're distracted and easily interrupted, you will not succeed.

So make it harder for yourself to be interrupted. Your best results come from times when you are completely focused on

---

1   Paul Atchley, "You Can't Multitask, so Stop Trying," *Harvard Business Review*, July 23, 2014, https://hbr.org/2010/12/you-cant-multi-task-so-stop-tr.

and engaged in what matters to you. You don't want to be interrupted during those important moments. Put your phone on airplane mode or in another room, or power it off completely. Turn off notifications. If you're in an office, put a sign on the door that says, "Focusing for the next thirty minutes—do not disturb." You need to set boundaries to make yourself uninterruptible, because your attention is your most valuable asset. You will avoid burnout by protecting your attention and focus. Remember that people pay you big bucks for your attention.

Other ways to manage your attention include outsourcing your email inbox to your executive assistant and making sure you are unsubscribed from every list that sends you things you are not interested in.

We upgrade our phones frequently, but we rarely upgrade our minds. Focus is a muscle—train it like one. Don't flex distraction muscles and unconscious thoughts as you scroll; only use technology for purposes that further your goals. Fire can cook food, but it can also burn your house down. Similarly, technology and devices with the potential to distract us can be good or bad depending on how they're used. The number one cause of distraction is the device in your hand.

Don't outsource your feelings to your devices and become dependent and reliant on them. If you place your emotions and feelings into all the things that happen on your phone instead of forging real connections with people, life will pass you by. The metaverse and virtual reality are on the rise, which is very exciting. But humans still will also need real, in-person connections. There are so many mental health benefits to not becoming isolated phone zombies and instead maintaining our ability to deal with people. Think about the generation who is under twenty-one years old today. Do you think many of them have excellent in-person communication skills? In my experience, if they've grown up mostly interacting with others from behind a keyboard, they don't. I've seen this play out the most when I interview young people and college students, usually around age eighteen to twenty-one, for internships. You can tell that it's not just the experience of communicating in person that they lack, but also a degree of comfort in those situations that does not serve them well.

People say, "I don't have time for _____," whether it's not having time for exercise, dates with their spouse, reading to their children, pursuing a hobby, or finishing a project. You never have time for what you procrastinate or delay, but I guarantee if you check the usage on your cell phone, many hours of your day were lost in the black hole of distractions.

Attention management starts with setting personal boundaries, and most often those personal boundaries involve our use of our own smartphones. So many people say they're busy, but they spend six hours on their phone doing who knows what.

I spoke onstage in front of ten thousand high school students in 2019 with the late Collin Kartchner, the founder of Save the Kids Foundation. His whole mission was making kids and parents aware of the harmful effects of teen addiction to social media and smartphones. We spoke to ten thousand students in one day, and the messages he got were incredible. Kids said they deleted their Snapchat after feeling suicidal and planning to harm themselves soon due to depression. Just deleting the app lifted a huge burden and brought them a sense of relief and hope. Some of them had become accustomed to spending ten hours a day on their phone.

. . .

Technology addiction affects us all. Smartphones are an amazing tool for advancement, but they're also extremely dangerous and addictive. When it comes to managing attention, a smartphone, if used improperly, could ruin your whole life. Your attention is in demand and highly valuable. If you're wasting hours and hours a day in the black hole of your smartphone, you won't reach the fulfillment that you hope to reach. Connection is valuable if you're connected to the right people,

and technology can help. But conscious use is
a far cry from multitasking and wasting time.

. . .

COVID presented particular challenges for kids and people struggling with isolation. It's okay to be alone, but it's not okay to be lonely. Social isolation adds to stress and health challenges. We naturally crave human connection. If your emotional life only happens on your phone, you risk becoming dead to the world. It's dangerous. Instead of overreacting to what's on your phone, be fully present with the people in your real life.

LEVEL UP BY LETTING GO

Delegating to others and removing yourself from interruptions and decisions might seem like giving up control, but you actually gain control over your time and your attention to focus on the most important aspects of your life and business. "I delegate by hiring great people," Frank Murgic says. "I also use the 'who not how' concept in hiring the services of top professionals on a fractional basis."

In managing his attention, Vess Pearson says, "My secret is to invest in great people to help eliminate time-consuming work at home and work." His executive and personal assistant "are crucial for me to be productive and enable me to keep my focus where it needs to be. Together, they manage my schedule, keep me organized, and reduce the number of tasks that fill up my day."

Sometimes highly successful people let ego get in the way of sharing responsibilities with others. They think they should make all the decisions themselves, which is a mistake. Your contribution is your vision, not your opinion on every last nitty-gritty task. Get the right people on your team, give them the vision, outline the desired outcomes, and explain the purpose of their work—but don't get wrapped up in telling them how to do it or how to get there.

Finding their own best way of executing allows them to grow, develop, and learn. Successful people with big egos get in their own way by micromanaging their teams. They overdirect. Employees waste time waiting on them to say yes or no to everything.

Emilio Diez Barroso, the Chairman and CEO of NALA Investments who runs two family offices and is someone who prioritizes connection, contribution, and adventure in his life, says he hears a common phrase when talking about ego: "They say 'no one will do it like I do,'" he said. "But in reality, it's usually because identities get created, and our ego is very invested in not giving up what we perceive as the 'valuable' one."

Vishwas Choksi, Co-founder of Sports for All in India, said he takes a similar approach. "Since I am in the ever growing/ exponential mindset, I do not have time to micromanage," he said. "I always tell my teams to use me as a problem solver if they are stuck or confused with something. The key is to hire the correct top resources and let them run with what they have. My job as the entrepreneur is to create the systems, processes, policies, and culture that support this."

Many of my peers don't understand how I have the undistracted lifestyle I have while being involved in leading multiple businesses. They're still trying to do everything themselves and are less intentional with their attention, not willing to give up as much day-to-day control as I am. I started from a place of figuring out the least I could do in my business so I could maximize my attention on what matters most to me. I've eliminated 90 percent of what I was doing five years ago—I just don't do any of it anymore. The operations and specialized details of each person's role are not things I need to be sticking my nose in every day. As Steve Jobs said, "It doesn't make sense to hire smart people and then tell them what to do; we hire smart people so they can tell us what to do."

Before, I was always reacting and responding to everything coming at me. I was playing email ping-pong in my inbox all day and night. Now, I have significantly more free time to think, connect, and create. My peers are still mostly stuck in reactive mode. They're inundated with a barrage of interruptions and demands because they're unwilling to let go, set boundaries, be firm, and say no to what falls outside their core priorities.

In the last three years, I've gone completely hands-off with internal operations. I tell my team they know the best way to execute better than I do, so they should figure it out. That's why I've hired and trained them. Sometimes they come back to me and ask me which way to proceed, and I say I have no idea. I'm not going to tell them how to do it. I trust they will figure it out. Simon Sinek once said, "A boss who micromanages is like a coach who wants to get in the game. Leaders guide and support and then sit back and cheer from the sidelines." If you empower your people, you don't have to babysit every little detail and create a decision-making bottleneck in your business, as I'll explore more in the next chapter.

"Growth and control is an inverse relationship," according to Frank Murgic. "In my profession, pharmacists in general are perfectionists, which can lead to analysis paralysis. In order to grow, you have to let go."

Reimagining the control of your time and attention is an effective approach to lifestyle freedom across industries and passions. Even rapper Lil Wayne has commented on its impact on his life, saying, "I tried to pay attention, but attention paid me."

To climb a mountain successfully, you need to focus on the mountain you're climbing. You can't make progress if you're distracted by all the mountains you're not on, all the people who want you to help them climb a different mountain, or all the activities you could do that aren't mountain climbing. Commit to your current journey, based on your personal strengths and values, and find the right people to help you.

KEY TAKEAWAYS

- It can be hard to know what to say yes to and what to decline when you're so highly skilled. It's tempting to overcommit your time to opportunities that don't actually warrant your attention.

- Delegating to others and removing yourself from interruptions and decisions might seem like giving up control, but you actually gain control over your

time and your attention to focus on the most
important aspects of your life and business.

- Attention management is the practice of
controlling distractions, being present in the
moment, finding flow, and maximizing focus, so
that you can unleash your genius.

- Regardless of the demands on your time, you can
implement focused attention on the people you
care about. When was the last time you left your
phone in another room specifically to spend time
with those you care about? Try it today.

"Deciding what not to do is as important as deciding what to do."

—JESSICA JACKLEY

SIX

OWN, DON'T OPERATE

O wning rather than operating dovetails with managing your attention. Don't waste time trying to figure out how to do everything and insist on being both the visionary and the implementer of all decisions in your life. Instead, find the people who can help you do it, who you can hire to do it, or who can facilitate. You must be willing to trust the skills and abilities of others—and put your ego and obsession with control to the side. Allowing others space to grow frees your attention to do your most important work. Sharing control serves you, too, because you're more likely to win.

. . .

Owners can fall prey to control issues. It's
important to be willing to let go and not get
attached to the methods or the process. I have
an outcome goal, but I'm not attached to the
means of getting there. I'm open to admitting
I'm wrong. I'm open to admitting someone else
has a better idea than mine. Frankly, I don't
care how we reach the target. If you have a
faster and better way to get there, let's go.

. . .

I want my team members to take charge. I don't want to micromanage, because if I'm talking, I'm not learning. I don't just want to hear my own ideas again and again. Listening leads to learning through other perspectives and ideas.

I am a complete believer of Dan Sullivan's "who, not how" principle. In his book *Who Not How: The Formula to Achieve Bigger Goals Through Accelerating Teamwork*, Dan and Dr. Benjamin Hardy write:

It can be easy to focus on How, especially for high achievers who want to control what they can control, which is themselves. It takes vulnerability and trust to expand your efforts and build a winning team. It takes wisdom to recognize that 1) other people are more than capable enough to handle much of the Hows, and 2) that your efforts and contribution (your "Hows") should be focused exclusively where your greatest passion and impact are. Your attention and energy should not be spread thin, but purposefully directed where you can experience extreme flow and creativity.

If you're bogged down in the basic administrative work, you're not working on the larger vision. Clarify the vision and leave the execution to the experts. Micromanagers aren't efficient. Until you get out of your own way, you can't truly progress.

"Own, don't operate" refers to having an ownership equity stake in a business but not positioning yourself as the sole decision-maker or the day-to-day operator. You can make money without getting in everyone's way and telling them how to do their jobs. As an owner, you don't need every single piece of information before moving forward.

HANDS-OFF OWNERSHIP
EMPOWERS OTHERS

Last year, my company, Pacific Capital, hired a woman with an MBA who'd immigrated from Brazil. She was looking to really kick-start her business career in the US, and I gave her a chance by hiring her after she completed a brief internship. Within her first year, I gave her increased responsibilities and a promotion, doubling her income—and she completely broke down in tears.

Before telling her the news of her promotion and big salary raise, I'd asked her how she liked working at the company, what she liked about her job, and what her challenges were. She said she loved working with us because it "allows her to be her real self...finally." In the past internships and jobs, people micromanaged her. She had creative ideas, but they constrained her and told her what to do, so she couldn't fully succeed and implement her ideas. She said I set the vision while also giving her enough room and space to grow, which felt exciting to her. I communicated my trust in her to try things and improve along the way.

I really appreciated her feedback, because it captured exactly what I'm trying to do: create an environment where people will take more responsibility and own their role. They'll grow, be the operators, and make the decisions for the benefit of our clients and business. People rise to the level of the expectations placed on them. Owners impede their progress and the progress of those around them when they think they have the magic touch, need to make all the decisions, and must have the final say. We don't always know better. We should stay in our lane and let others stay in theirs. People who meaning-fully contribute to the work and outcomes are more invested.

. . .

"Great leaders do not create followers,
they create more leaders."
—Tom Peters

. . .

Mark Choe has had a similar experience: "Having a level of autonomy is one of the benefits people really enjoy about working with us. I try to focus on how I can support each department and get the departments in sync without getting in the way," he says. "I am still working off the idea that I always have to be the hardest working person in my business."

Owning rather than operating requires letting go of ego and setting boundaries. The two go hand in hand to protect your time and attention. Be an owner, not an operator. As inves-tors and equity owners, we get involved in many businesses. Learn where your participation brings value and where it's not necessary. Have the humility to not inject yourself into all aspects of the operations.

According to Craig Coppola, "One of the best things I have done and do on a daily basis is build self-managing teams for myself and my investments. This is critical to living the life you want and to have the success you are striving for. My life today is fantastic in large part to my partners and people on my team. Period." Like me, he builds things and gets out of the way. He isn't afraid to empower his team.

Mike Wandler shares, "Now I realize my teams want me to delegate everything possible. They want responsibility and the same freedoms I want: time, money, relationships, and purpose." The primary motivator for entrepreneurs is time and financial freedom, which you can only unlock when you let others run the operation. As Vess Pearson put it, "The main job of a CEO is to find the right people and develop culture. Everything else can be delegated."

KNOW WHAT YOU DON'T KNOW

Highly successful people often get caught up in thinking their way is the best way, because they're highly skilled in one area. I've had financial conversations with very successful doctors and surgeons, for instance, who think because they're so knowledgeable about surgery and healthcare, they're equally qualified in finance—but they're not. Wearing a white coat doesn't make them an expert in everything. They get caught up in pride because they've made a great deal of money. Wealthy people often think because they have money, they also have knowledge in all areas, but they don't.

. . .

"It ain't what you don't know that gets you into trouble. It's what you know for sure that just ain't so."
—Mark Twain

. . .

If you go beyond your expertise, you may not only slow down operations but actually have a detrimental impact. What you say as an owner carries weight, and if your input is wrong, it can get the team off track. As an owner, you're not there full-time. The people on the ground are often more in touch with what's going on and what is needed to fix the issues, as long as they have clarity on your overarching vision. Don't confuse them with misleading suggestions or by inserting yourself in the mix. Stay out of it and make your highest, best impact with your own areas of expertise. Don't be a part-time manager or an operator—be an owner.

Being a visionary and creating big opportunities for growth is more important than having your hands in everything. Grasping that concept is a challenge when you're used to being the main character and decision-maker in the room, with everyone looking to you for approval, direction, and the final say in so many different areas of your life. You get asked to be the keynote speaker. You sit on the board of the non-profit. People want your input in all the important decisions. As a result, it's very easy to get your hands entangled in way too many decisions.

. . .

Freedom comes from admitting you're successful in certain areas but you don't know everything. When you acknowledge the limits of your expertise, you stop wasting your time trying to control everything when your energy, attention, and resources could be better spent elsewhere. You can focus on building an amazing team that handles the day-to-day concerns instead of trying to be a part-time expert in a hundred things.

. . .

INVEST MONEY, NOT TIME

The Draft Sports Complex is a business I'd always wanted to start. Friends and I talked about having a large sports complex in our region of Southern California that could host national tournaments for basketball, volleyball, and other sports, serving as a gathering place for thousands of people.

It's an arena for celebrating student athletes and children who want to play sports. I'm passionate about it because my wife and I have five kids, and we're a sports-obsessed family of athletes.

I wanted to create that business but didn't remotely have any time to operate it. I was fortunate enough to get together and partner with a few people who were also interested in bringing the complex to the community. We started multiple travel club sports programs for boys and girls and now have over fifty teams as part of our business. We also have the facility that is their home court: the Draft Sports Complex, a seventy-five-thousand-square-foot building that is home to many national and regional sports tournaments and is full of young student athletes practicing and training from morning until late at night. I agreed to be a co-founder and financial investor, as well as an advisor to give the team business and financial advice. My contribution was money and expertise, but not time—I've never operated the business and am not involved in any day-to-day decisions.

I can contribute expertise and financial resources when the business needs it, but I won't be giving any time to operate it. My co-founders went into the venture with the understanding they'd handle the operations and have offices there to oversee the day-to-day. They make the phone calls, send the emails, set up the tournaments, and build the business with their time and effort. My contribution was expertise, ideas, and financial backing, but almost zero time and effort. The combination has led to the success of the business.

Over time, the bigger your businesses get and the more involved and connected you get, the more obligations you have your hands in. Your situation can get completely out of balance. When you're extremely involved in so many different areas, you get good at being dependable but can overcommit. When you're spread too thin, it's impossible to give your highest and best self to any one thing, so you need to prioritize.

Saying yes to too many things causes us to be overobligated and therefore less effective and less focused. The real way to create value at a high level is to ensure the value-creation proposition doesn't require your presence.

If you feel you need to be involved in everything, then you'll always be tethered to your phone. It will be the chain around your ankle when you're on your family vacation, at your daughter's graduation ceremony, or in any other meaningful moment. You'll think you're so important that you have to be making decisions even during those important life events. Your attention will be on your phone instead of in the moment, because you haven't decided to completely step back and just own. There are massive costs to the belief you need your hands in every decision.

"Own, don't operate" applies to your investments too. Don't be Mr. Joe Operator showing up to work at 7:00 a.m. and sweeping the floor. Own your investments, but don't tinker with them. Partner with a trusted fiduciary family office to help implement your financial strategy and goals' implementation. You don't need your hands involved in every day-to-day decision. Own your portfolio just like you'd own any other cash-flowing business. Let the pros you've hired exercise their expert judgment, and free up your time for your higher purposes. It's no different from any other business ownership and delegation.

USE YOUR IP TO CREATE
PROCESSES AND SYSTEMS

To ensure you can delegate successfully and own rather than operate, you need to create systems, processes, and workflows. Assemble a team. Get the great ideas out of your head, formalize them with your team, and trademark them. I've trademarked more than ten different processes I invented at Pacific Capital, such as our Financial Life Inspection® process. I trademarked the phrase "Smart, Not Spoiled,"™ as well as the twelve financial planning processes my firm offers.[2] We have an incredible patent attorney who special-izes in intellectual property (IP) for privately held businesses.

I developed a way of helping the families of entrepreneurs verbalize plans they'd never spoken out loud before by ask-ing good questions. We take them through a process of fig-uring out their most important goals and priorities, writing them down, and creating a plan to investigate what they're doing well, what they need help with, and which professional experts are best suited to help them. As a result, I became one of the top financial advisors in the country.

The challenge is there's only one of me, and I only have so much time. I can't replicate my services and advice if it's all in my head and based on instinct and practice. So I had to create unique processes and systems and trademark them, and then hire and teach people (who have much more tech-nical expertise than me anyways) to use them. That ground-work has allowed me to own and not operate—or lead

2 • Financial Life Inspection®
• Strategy Conversation®
• The Family Finance Centralizer™
• The Family Protection Advantage™
• The Tax Mitigation Method™
• The Investment Strategy Enhancer™
• The Legacy Transfer Advantage™
• The Business Ownership Navigator™
• Goals Conversation®
• The Financial Freedom Formula™
• The Cash Flow Maximizer™
• The Giving Formula™
• The Real Estate ROI Snapshot™

without being involved in every company meeting or every client meeting. I could help many more people by getting out of my own way.

PRO TIP

Don't just delegate and systemize processes that work well in your organization: trademark them, hire and teach people to use them, and step out of the way. This small act is one that's relatively simple, but there's a big payoff if you can do it well.

Keegan Caldwell, Founder and Managing Attorney at Caldwell IP (one of the fastest growing law firms in America) states that developing intellectual property and using it as a business asset has other great benefits as well. "You can significantly increase the value of your business with IP," he said. "There's a reason that nearly 85 percent of the value of the S&P 500 is intangible assets. Founders and executives can make a tremendous impact on their enterprise value by using intellectual property correctly."

By formalizing the processes and sharing them with our team, I can expand my vision to reach exponentially more people than if I stayed involved in all the internal operations.

By stepping back, I leveled up. I believe I'm best at having conversations with people one-on-one and helping them uncover their financial and life goals, and then helping them create the plan and see the clear path to achieve those goals. The question became how I could get that skill outside myself and teach others to excel at it as well. With the right training, they could be as good as or hopefully even better than me.

If you're the best at what you do, it doesn't mean you have to do it all. Your ego and overinvolvement can hold you back. Focus on how to get great people to do great work, to scale your vision, and help others grow. Great leaders can step back and support others in being successful. As Donald Walters says, "The greatest leader is not necessarily the one who does the greatest things. The great leader is the one that gets people to do the greatest things."

. . .

A true leader lifts everyone around them by setting the vision, teaching, training, and then stepping back with the willingness to relinquish the spotlight. Trademarking your processes offers a practical, tactical idea so you can continue to reap the benefits of the skills that made you successful as you teach others to practice them as well.

. . .

Given all your experience, you have significant intellectual property inside your head. Not putting a stamp on it is almost shameful. It's a waste. You can share it and make it permanent in the world instead of keeping it inside. You're the only one who can deliver your expertise. Expand your contribution without expanding the day-to-day effort you expend.

One of the reasons I felt inspired to write books is to share more insights and experience with a wider global audience. If these experiences and knowledge could only be shared one appointment at a time, I wouldn't make nearly the same impact. Instead, I've sold books all over the world and helped families globally, which is just one of the great results of stepping back and thinking bigger.

DO LESS TO ACHIEVE MORE

Strategic Coach has a concept called Unique Ability™ (UA)—essentially, an activity that keeps you fascinated and motivated that keeps you fired up, your sweet spot. One of my unique abilities is connecting with people and building relationships. I help people talk about their goals and envision and plan for a better, more exciting future. I am also comfortable with public speaking and consider it a unique ability. One of my wife's unique abilities is building, fixing, and crafting with her hands. Assembling something with a lot of parts and a long instruction manual stresses me out and drains my energy. To her, it's easy and no big deal. Speaking onstage in front of ten thousand people seems fun and not stressful at all to me. But to her, she'd be losing sleep all week ahead of that speech.

UA is something that comes naturally to you; it's what you're called to do. God put you on Earth with these innate, incredible talents; you may not think they're a big deal, but others could never replicate them. My friend Julia Waller is an author, a coach, and the Unique Ability Specialist at Strategic Coach. She offers an incredible program for people to dive deep into their own unique abilities and to create an action plan to do more of what brings them joy and less of what drains their energy. I went through Julia's program in March 2020 and can truly say that it changed my life.

UA relates to the need to delegate and outsource everything except the few things you're naturally, exceptionally good at and truly enjoy. By doing so, you'll make the biggest possible impact and will be more filled with excitement and high levels of energy.

In reflecting on why high achievers often struggle to give up control, Justin Dalton says they "often want their 'fingerprints' on every aspect of the venture they're involved in, which is a blessing and a curse." Over time, he has "learned to focus on what I am absolute best at and where I produce the most measurable results while weeding out projects/items that are just background 'noise' in the larger scheme of things."

His emphasis on measurability can be motivating, because you can lean into your nature of increasing the most important metrics rather than focusing on what you're giving up. Learning how to delegate and own instead of operate frees you up to fulfill your highest, best purpose: climbing the mountains you were meant to climb, and leaving a legacy in the process.

KEY TAKEAWAYS

- "Own, don't operate" refers to having an ownership equity stake in a business but not positioning yourself as the sole decision-maker or the day-to-day operator.

- Owning rather than operating requires letting go of ego and setting boundaries. The two go hand in hand to protect your time and attention. Learn where your participation brings value and where it's not necessary. Have the humility to not inject yourself into all aspects of the operations.

- You can't replicate your service if it's all in your head and based on instinct and practice. Pursue trademarks and build repeatable processes.

- Harness what you're exceptionally good at and truly enjoy (also called your "Unique Ability"). This way, you'll make the biggest possible impact, will be more filled with excitement, and have high levels of energy.

"When I let go of what I am,
I become what I might be."

—LAO TZU

SEVEN

DON'T STOP: YOU AREN'T FINISHED

Once you've arrived at the top, it's easy to stick with what you know and stay there. It's a comfortable place to be in. Not only have you found your proper lane, but you're leading the chase within it. It would be easy to cruise along your same route and routine without ever mixing it up.

· · ·

If you've reached the level of achievement we're talking about in this book, you've already put in your time on the struggle bus. You grinded out those early years to get to this point, and you're done with the beginner phase. You're an expert, thought leader, and influencer in your space. What, then, is the big deal about trying something new? Why would you want to go back *through the hard times of not knowing what you're doing, potentially falling or failing?*

. . .

The answer is simple: because that's where all the magic happens. All progress takes place outside of your comfort zone. I love this quote by Jane Pauley: "The courage to try something new makes me proud." For me, the root of that pride she is speaking of is finding new opportunities that will stretch and help you grow in different ways.

Brian Tracy famously said, "You can only grow if you are willing to feel awkward and uncomfortable trying something new." In other words, keep a beginner's mind.

REJECT THE STATUS QUO

You've never settled for keeping the status quo. When you chose to create this lifestyle of abundance, you rejected everything that the masses would accept as "normal." The status quo is boring.

Dr. Jordan Metzl, a sports medicine physician at New York's Hospital for Special Surgery, told the *Wall Street Journal*: "Trying something new that shakes up your routine can really give you a fresh perspective and get you excited."

In Jared Hess's comedy sensation *Napoleon Dynamite*, there's a middle-aged character named Uncle Rico. One of Uncle Rico's favorite things to talk to his nephews about in the film was how his high school football team would've won state...if *only* they'd have put him in the game. His character is absolutely fixated on that one moment from decades ago.

While maybe not to *that* extreme, we all know people who are completely past-focused. I'm going to bet the names coming into your mind aren't people you feel energized by or want to spend too much time with, right? That type of mindset or person is not anything you want a part of in your life. Deciding to rest on your laurels by putting yourself on cruise control is contrary to your DNA as an entrepreneur. According to Louise Perry, "Life is change. If you aren't growing and evolving, you're standing still, and the rest of the world is surging ahead."

. . .

Don't be seduced by the success in your past.
Reach forward for what you can do, not backward

*to what you already have done. You still can get
energized and excited by new opportunities ahead.*

. . .

As Dan Sullivan says, "Make sure you always see your future
as bigger and better than your past." If you're always the
wealthiest and smartest person in the room, you're never
truly challenging yourself. This can have real consequences,
even health ones. The Alzheimer's Association includes "challenge and activate your mind" on its list of "ten ways to love
your brain."[3] In addition, Harvard Health reported the following in 2021:

> Your brain has the ability to learn and grow as you age—a
> process called brain plasticity—but for it to do so, you
> have to train it on a regular basis.

> "Eventually, your cognitive skills will wane and thinking
> and memory will be more challenging, so you need to
> build up your reserve," says Dr. John N. Morris, director of
> social and health policy research at the Harvard-affiliated
> Institute for Aging Research. "Embracing a new activity

---

3 "10 Ways to Love Your Brain," Alzheimer's Association, accessed July
   21, 2022, https://www.alz.org/help-support/brain_health/10_ways_to_
   love_your_brain

that also forces you to think and learn and requires ongoing practice can be one of the best ways to keep the brain
healthy."[4]

What we know about the connection between keeping your
mind sharp through challenging it and overall health benefits is different now than it was twenty years ago. *Everything*
is different now than it was twenty years ago. The speed of
change in technology and how the world works requires you
to stay sharp and learn new things all the time. If you're too
set in your ways, you'll become obsolete. You'll be stuck on a
plateau while everyone else continues to climb.

PRO TIP

Pick one thing you always wanted to learn but never
did—a hobby, a sport, an instrument, a language—and
set aside "learning time" or "beginner time." Whether or
not you become an expert in what you choose is not the
point. Instead, notice what it feels like when you allow
yourself to be completely and utterly a beginner.

---

4 "Train Your Brain," Harvard Health Publishing, February 15, 2021,
   https://www.health.harvard.edu/mind-and-mood/train-your-brain

KEEP LEARNING TO KEEP GROWING

As an entrepreneur, you are already very comfortable with uncertainty. You know that great opportunities require some level of uncertainty, risk, and new learning. You've learned to make big decisions and move ahead despite not knowing the outcome. Having a beginner's mind helps in these cases, allowing you to be more curious and open-minded, willing to try things and get feedback that will help you make adjustments and get better. You'll see opportunities you would have missed with blinders on. A byproduct of this approach is that, as you go, you're flexing your humility muscle.

Why does that matter? Because when you go back to being a rookie, you have to ask for advice and guidance. You admit you still don't know everything about everything. When you're willing to *not* be the expert, it makes you a stronger and deeper resource for everyone around you. There is more of you to give if there's more invested in you, making you a better parent, partner, and so on.

Lee Richter, official member at Forbes Business Council and CEO of Holistic Veterinary Care, says:

Why a beginner's mind? It is so we can imagine the way things could be: even better. Once an idea emerges, our

mind can take it to the next level, and with the right col-
laborators at the right time, we can take the idea and
launch it into something that never existed before. It is
exciting to create at this level!

A beginner's mind allows us to see the step-by-step process
and then inspires us to create an improved process for others to join in. It's how Disney got started...he visited a park
called Children's Fairyland in Oakland California, and he
was inspired to take an idea and make it even better by
creating a special lifestyle experience with Disneyland and
Disney World. He used his beginner's mind along with
real inspiration to create something the world had never
experienced up to that point. It's a fascinating journey for
those willing to do the work to make it happen.

Personally, I am a voracious reader, a consumer of podcasts,
and love to participate in groups with people who are far
smarter and wealthier than me. I surround myself with big
thinkers as much as possible and ask them as many questions as they're willing to answer. When I look back ten years,
I can see I've been on an exponential curve of seeking to learn
from other people.

But even I need reminding about stepping out of our routine
every once in a while. My wife is great about that, especially

when it comes to travel. If it were up to me, I'd go to the same island or vacation spots every year because they are familiar and I know that we love these places, but she insists on picking a brand-new place to visit each time. She always wants to explore parts of the world that we've never seen. Some of the best moments of my life have been with my family on trips just like that, outside our comfort zone, experiencing something completely new together.

. . .

Always remain open to learning new things.
If you don't learn, you don't grow.

. . .

Dan Sullivan says, "When you stop learning new things, developing new ideas, and meeting new people, you accelerate the aging process. If you're no longer growing and no longer useful, you're sending powerful signals to your mind and body—not to mention the people around you—that it's time to slow down."

There are tangible benefits to beginning again and again too. With most industries—probably yours—changing rapidly, being a learn-it-all and not a know-it-all will help you capitalize on those changes instead of fall victim to them.

The gig economy. Digital finance. Cryptocurrency. 3-D printing. E-commerce. Free/unlimited information online.

These things changed everything—and the only thing we know for certain is that there are more changes on the way. Being flexible and open-minded gives us a better chance of coming out of those shifts with the upper hand.

. . .

"In the beginner's mind there are many possibilities.
In the expert's mind there are few."
—Shunryu Suzuki

. . .

As Dr. Ben Hardy said, "Research shows that your future self will be a different person than you. However, research also shows that most people assume that who they are now is, for the most part, who they will always be. In other words, people assume their future self won't be much different from their current self. In other words, most people have a fixed mindset—which means they've overly committed to and overly defined their current self. Having a beginner's mind means you know your current self is temporary and limited, and that you know you can and will change. This allows an unlimited mindset where you're not trying to prove yourself, but always seeking to learn more and outgrow your current ignorance."

Doing this takes vulnerability, and I understand that when you're held in such high regard, it's harder to appear vulnerable. However, when you express clearly what you are unsure about and what you're seeking help or advice on, your vulnerability actually attracts much more help. Nobody wants to rush to help someone who already "knows it all." Be willing to ask others for help, insights, advice, and introductions. Often, those leaders who continue learning and seeking help are those who have the most success.

SAY LESS

Oliver Wendell Holmes Jr. said, "A mind that is stretched by a new experience can never go back to its old dimensions."

There are two great ways to facilitate that stretch: ask questions or say nothing and just listen. That's why I find that when I'm in groups of really smart and wealthy people, the wisest people are saying the least.

I recently went to a small group Strategic Coach conference in Chicago with Gino Wickman, the Founder of EOS Worldwide and an author of many of my favorite books for entrepreneurs. He is, of course, an icon for the operating system he created that helped millions of entrepreneurs, but what impressed me the most wasn't that. It was that in every situation I was in with him—at lunch, over breakout sessions—he asked thoughtful, open-ended questions. And then he listened—a lot. It wasn't what he said, but what he didn't say. He was an engaged listener and was even taking notes as if each answer was very important to him.

Ask yourself: When was the last time you learned something for the first time?

Make it today.

KEY TAKEAWAYS

- When you're incredibly successful in one or two specific arenas, it can be easy to cruise along your same route(s) and routine(s) without ever mixing it up.

- All progress takes place outside of your comfort zone. Find new opportunities that will stretch and help you grow in different ways.

- Not only is having a beginner's mind good from personal and professional agility standpoints, but research also shows that learning new things is very literally one of the top ten things you can do to keep your brain healthy as you age.

- Be willing to ask others for help, insights, advice, and introductions. Often, those leaders who continue learning and seeking help are those who have the most success.

"The purpose of life is
a life of purpose."

—ROBERT BYRNE

EIGHT

NEVER RETIRE

Retirement is dead, at least in the original, traditional sense. High-achieving entrepreneurs do not turn into the people sitting in a rocking chair on the porch, reading the newspaper or watching the news for hours on end. That's just not who you are. You're not going to stop working cold turkey at age sixty-five like your grandparents or great-grandparents. And that's a good thing. Staying in motion keeps you healthy and active.

. . .

If you sell your business in a huge exit, the payday will forever change your life financially. The challenge then is, **now what?** *Once you*

have the money and have descended from the
mountain, should you just chill on the beach and
do nothing for the rest of your life? No chance.

. . .

That plan is a recipe for disaster and misery. You got where you are by being the Energizer Bunny who keeps going and creating and building. You have more ideas to offer. Slamming on your brakes or hitting "stop" and never reentering the game is a highly unhealthy choice. And it won't work with your personality anyway.

. . .

You didn't work your entire career on an assembly
line in a manufacturing plant for decades until your
back gave out, and now it's time to rest and "retire."
Most of your success and money have been made
from your neck up. You're not a laborer; you're a
visionary, a thought leader. To shut off that muscle
and never exercise it again by retiring is a dangerous
choice and a recipe for quick misery. The literal
definition for "retire" is: "to retreat, to go back, to
withdraw towards seclusion, to take out of circulation
and usefulness." Does that sound appealing to you?
Knowing what type of person you are, I highly doubt it.

. . .

In the US, we have been taught that retirement is what you get at the end of the race, and it is about how you entertain yourself from the point when the race is over until you die. I've known many people who tried to retire completely, and after six months or a year, they were nothing but antsy and unhappy. They felt unproductive and like they were no longer useful. They had a drive to create, lead, and inspire. Turning off that switch left them floundering and languishing. They didn't know what to do anymore, and that lack of purpose and direction harmed their mental and physical health. Retirement makes more sense if you really dread what you do for work.

Do not follow the traditional path of retirement. You're wired to stay engaged. You took a different path to get where you are today, so you must take a different path in your future. What the rest of the world is suggesting does not apply to you. Face it; don't fight it.

FIND PURPOSE BEYOND THE MONEY

You're not motivated just by money. What really motivates you is the freedom that money creates. The freedom to do whatever you want, whenever you want, with whomever you want. Once you have enough money, you still want to create, engage, and have a purpose. If you aren't working for the money, you still need to find meaning in your day. Maybe that means getting more involved in charitable causes or sitting on the board of a nonprofit or different companies you're excited about. You might start a business with a younger family member or friend to mentor them. Once you cash out or once your business is completely running and growing on its own, you enter a new era of choice and freedom, and what you do with that opportunity is extremely important. You must stay engaged.

PRO TIP

Instead of traditional retirement, reinvent yourself to start an entirely different company in a different industry. Tap into your network, experience, and knowledge to chart a new path. Continue your education. Travel. Choose a select few to mentor. Join the board of a nonprofit.

Do *something* that fuels your soul.

Many highly successful people stay in the game by serving on boards or as advisors. They seed startups or invest in growing venture-backed companies. That involvement keeps them excited and allows them to use their business experience without getting tied to the day-to-day operations of the business. I often see them start completely new businesses, building upon the experience they gained in their last successful business. Whatever you choose, make sure you continue to manage your attention and only say yes to opportunities that align with your priorities. You should have more freedom in "retirement," not less.

Part of my role is having conversations with people about what they want to do next once they've achieved total financial and time freedom. What are the best uses of your talents? What gets you excited? What gives you energy versus what drains you? What did you do in the last ten years before your business sale? Make a list of what you enjoyed and what you never want to do again, so you're clear on what you want when new possibilities arise.

. . .

Fulfillment is being able to do the things that bring you energy and joy, be with the people you care about, participate in meaningful activities, and have meaningful conversations, without the stress of operating a business or worrying about finances. Once you've reached a high level of financial freedom and independence, you don't need to think about money anymore. It's time to use your vision for a higher purpose.

. . .

RETIREMENT IS DEAD

Dan Sullivan wrote an article called "Why I Don't Believe in Retirement." He says retirement by its very definition means "no longer useful." He says, "We retire old machinery. We retire old clothing, and we retire old ideas because they stopped serving their purpose." While retirement made sense when the bulk of workers made a living with their bodies, it's not applicable to a high achiever like you. You've enjoyed the journey, so it's not a reward to hang up your hiking boots.

The only barriers preventing you from working into your sixties, seventies, and eighties are society's expectations and your own. Sullivan says by virtue of pursuing the entrepreneurial path:

> You've already declared independence from the boring world, the repetitive world, the usual world, the traditional path. And that means you've also declared independence from society's expectations, including the ones about what it means to get older...If you're no longer growing, no longer learning, no longer useful, you're sending power-ful signals to your mind and your body and to the people around you that it's time to slow down...You can choose a future that's always bigger and better than your path. Don't talk yourself into being taken out of use. Don't talk yourself into dying early.

American author Robert Byrne was famously quoted as saying, "The purpose of life is a life of purpose." That aligns with my philosophy, and I've seen it in my practice.

Traditionally, people will financially plan for *How soon can I finally quit this crappy path that I'm on?* What kind of way of living is that? That's not the lifestyle you chose. The entrepreneur, by virtue of going their own route and opting out of the system, has left that matrix. They don't need to get in line, work at a place they don't enjoy working, and do what they're told for thirty or forty years, and then retire and finally start to enjoy life. If you are a thought leader who is used to creating, it's dangerous to plan on completely shutting off your mind. The problem is, we don't hear much advice for the next phase in life for people like us. Traditional "retirement planning" advice does not apply to us at all.

Nothing you've ever done has been the traditional path, so traditional retirement won't fit you either. People love to talk about retirement planning, but what about my client who sold his business for $800 million in his forties? Before he came to us, he went to a financial services company that had him fill out a little one-page retirement planning questionnaire. He couldn't help but laugh, because none of it related to him at all. He didn't even understand it and couldn't relate to any of the questions.

Only a few percent of people are entrepreneurs, and an even smaller number reach the level of success to sell their business for hundreds of millions of dollars. If you are fortunate enough to be in this group, you need your own playbook and cannot rely on advice given to the masses.

I told our client who sold his multihundred-million-dollar business in his forties that he couldn't get wealth and life planning advice from employees of the big banks and people who don't personally understand the entrepreneur's mind. If you are an entrepreneur with many businesses who also invests in real estate, cryptocurrencies, startups, etc., should you really be going to get advice from someone who has little or no personal experience in any of that? If you are planning to transform your health and fitness, you wouldn't hire a personal trainer that does not personally eat healthy or work out themselves, would you? If you're seeking parenting advice for dealing with small children or struggling teenagers, you'd likely be looking for advice from people who are parents themselves, who've successfully navigated those stages of parenting.

There is a big difference in working with a travel agent and a personal travel guide. A travel agent is trying to sell you a vacation package on the phone from an office somewhere. It's a very transactional relationship and they most likely have not been on the excursion, visited the hotel, or gone on that vacation themselves personally. A travel guide is someone who literally goes with you, shows you the way, and gives insights on the journey because they've personally walked this exact path many times. Because of your wealth and success, you will forever have "travel agents" chasing you down trying to sell you the next piece of financial advice. They'll be the ones wanting to do a quick calculation of the age at which you can "retire," how much money you can take out of your investment accounts when you retire, when you'll die, and how much money you'll leave to your kids and grandkids after you die based on your "retirement plan." That's the lame, cookie-cutter, straight-off-the-shelf financial planning based on generic software that 99 percent of "advisors" do. That's working with a travel agent.

My clients don't care about those concerns. That standard advice doesn't apply to them. They aren't worried about withdrawing $5,000 versus $10,000 or even $50,000 a month. They're way past that common worry of having enough to be comfortable. They're not the people scared of running out of money before they die. As a result, they need to think very differently about what to do next with their time and their wealth, and whether "retirement" is even a thing that interests them. (Hint: most of the time, it's not.)

Watching the clock and enduring your work until you're sixty-five years old is not really living at all. I feel sad when

I see people approach work in that way, because it doesn't have to be like that. That mindset is a spillover from the 1940s and '50s. It's a mindset of assembly-line work, treating people like machines: how much we can squeeze out of a body before it's no longer useful. In the Information Age with rapidly evolving technology, where the majority of people are knowledge workers, we have more flexibility and freedom than we used to.

The game has completely changed, but people are still reading the old rulebook for directions and guidance, which is crazy to me. It's like looking at the Thomas Guide maps for driving directions and ignoring readily available GPS technology. Too many entrepreneurs are looking to the wrong people for advice, people who don't understand them at all. You've never paid attention to the advice and guidance of the traditional workforce in your life, so why start once you've reached the top of the mountain? Don't listen to someone who's never laced up their hiking boots and made that steep mountain climb themselves.

CHOOSING YOUR NEXT CLIMB

Given all the summits you've reached, can you imagine never hiking and climbing again, just sitting at the base of the mountain and thinking about your past? How extremely unfulfilling. Once you've gotten there, your legs are strong. You've acquired the mental toughness and experience to make it to the top. This is the strongest you've ever been. Keep climbing, and teach others how to climb. Don't go back to the playbook written by people who've never climbed a mountain to get advice on your next journey.

Simon Sinek reminds us about the importance of centering our life on our purpose in his best-selling book, *Start with Why*. He writes, "Working hard for something we do not care about is called stress, working hard for something we love is called passion. All organizations start with WHY, but only the great ones keep their WHY clear year after year. Those who forget WHY they were founded show up to the race every day to outdo someone else instead of to outdo themselves. The pursuit, for those who lose sight of WHY they are running the race, is for the medal or to beat someone else."

. . .

Purpose has to be the leading driver of your decisions about what to do next. Maybe your original purpose was to make an impact and achieve complete financial freedom for you and your family. Now that you've reached that financial independence and

will never worry about money again, what do
you care about? What really matters to you?
Where can you make the most impact?

. . .

"Research shows you are happier, healthier, perform better at work, and live a longer life when you give to a greater purpose," Vess Pearson says. "I'm very loyal to serving a greater purpose. I dedicate at least fifteen hours per week to service. I make time for it and am deliberate about it."

I have a friend who's a very successful ophthalmologist. He's gone to Africa multiple times and done tens of thousands of free surgeries, because the cause matters to him. Part of his life's calling is to help people who could never afford the kind of surgeries he does for a living. There's so much you can do with what you've learned and to stay fulfilled and keep your energy high. Find what means the most to you. The answer won't be the same for everyone.

Maybe you've always wanted to try something completely different. Now's the time. If money were no object, what would you love to do with your time? When you answer that question truthfully, you learn what genuinely matters to you. Ask yourself why a few times in a row to get more clarity and dig deeper. When you uncover what you really love to do, engage with it. It will give you more purpose, whether it's related to or completely different from whatever your primary business or career was.

"Impact is the most important thing to me," says Mark Choe. "I want the peace of mind knowing that I did my best to leave the world better off than I found it in the most significant way as I can. And the second thing is that I just love the creative game of business."

I'm an advocate of having personal mission statements for yourself and your family. It's critical to have something you're aiming for, something that guides you like a north star. Otherwise, you'll struggle to decide how to use your time and attention. It will be tempting to dabble instead of deeply committing to something fulfilling.

Figuring out what you want and want to do is an essential task, which you can learn more about in my first book, *Stress-Free Money*. Everything starts with a clear intention and well-defined goals. Once you meet your first tier of goals, you have a restart. Now you need to set the intention for the next phase of your journey. It's time to reset and define specific goals and mission statements based on what's important to you.

Casey Adams, Head of E-Commerce Logistics for North America at Maersk, who previously sold his company for nearly $1 billion dollars, said, "Our focus today is making sure our kids turn out to be incredible people. They need to find causes they're passionate about and find ways to make the world a better place. Charitable giving is a core value of our family. We've spoken with their kids about what's important to them and what charities to get involved with, and we created a donor advised fund (DAF)."

Many clients will create a donor-advised fund or a charitable foundation that their family and their extended family can get involved in to direct money, time, and attention to causes that they really care about. It's more active giving than passive giving. The purpose is giving to causes and nonprofits that you care about and directing money, services, and attention to those areas.

SHAPE YOUR LEGACY

I frequently think about the saying "It's important to make a dollar, but even more important to make a difference." Everything you're doing contributes to your legacy. Achieving time and lifestyle freedom is in service of fulfilling that legacy. When you consider the impact larger than yourself, beyond the financial metrics, you can proceed with purpose.

I continually think about my legacy because my wife and I have five kids and we are a purpose-driven family. I wrote my last book, *Smart, Not Spoiled*, because I care what happens to the future generations of my family. Financial literacy for children is not really a part of Pacific Capital, but it's something I care deeply about personally. It's a mission for me to bring financial literacy to families all over the world. I am taking that a step further with GravyStack, a financial app for kids that I co-founded with Scott Donnell and Travis Adams. I hope that financial content and learning from GravyStack will be part of my legacy of building financial competency for the next generation. On top of that, when I consider my legacy, I want to leave behind our family values of loving God and loving other people of all backgrounds. My legacy will include service, kindness, treating people the way they deserve to be treated, doing good, and using my time, talents, and money to do good locally and globally.

I look for ways to use abundance to be an uplifter, a giver, a builder, and a connector. I want my life's contribution to leave a permanent and positive impact for many people around the world. It is my hope that I've instilled similar goals in my kids that they will pass on to their kids. I'm leaving footprints on the mountain for future generations. Mike Wandler put a great spin on legacy and purpose by setting up a trust for education and entrepreneurship for his posterity:

"It is funded with $150,000, and they can draw down to $75,000 leaving the other money to grow while invested. This seed money to get them started has resulted in seven out of the seven of our descendants owning their own business."

My wife and I often receive compliments about our kids' good character, which is hugely gratifying to me. We often hear how welcoming, inclusive, grateful, and humble they are. All five are uniquely different, but they've been taught to be appreciative and generous to people of all backgrounds and circumstances. The last thing we'd want for our kids is for them to develop any kind of arrogance or spoiled ingratitude. In our family, we believe it's possible to achieve great success and still treat everyone with respect and kindness. Being at the pinnacle doesn't require belittling people on the ground. Nothing we have will go with us in the end anyway.

My dad is much more risk-averse than I am. He's not as much of a risk-taker but is rather conservative in his financial and business decisions. Still, he was CEO of a national egg company that did over a billion dollars in annual revenue. He's fluent in Spanish from his two-year volunteer service mission in Buenos Aires, Argentina. As the CEO, he would go to the warehouses and plants across the country and speak Spanish to all the warehouse workers and entry-level employees making minimum wage. He'd get to know their names. They loved him because he treated them with humanity and spoke their language. They told him many times how that made them feel important and recognized. I learned so much about leadership from his example.

I've never heard my dad talk negatively about anyone in my life, and I'm forty-three. That's pretty remarkable. My mom is the same way. Her legacy will be one of determination and integrity. My parents' and grandparents' examples remind me of my WHY in all that I do as a business man and a family man, a community member, and a public servant. In the end, the most important investments we make aren't measured in dollars and cents, but in impact. My family set that example for me, and now my wife and I set it for our own children. We know that no matter what mountains we may face and attempt to conquer in this life, the climb is so much sweeter together.

KEY TAKEAWAYS

- Challenge what you know about the concept of "retirement." It's not in the DNA of a high-achieving entrepreneur to stop cold turkey at age sixty-five and sit in a rocking chair for the rest of your life.

- Only a few percent of people are entrepreneurs, and an even smaller number reach the level of success to sell their business for hundreds of millions of dollars. If you are fortunate enough to be in this group, you need your own playbook and cannot rely on advice given to the masses.

- Ask yourself: If money were no object, what would you love to do with your time? When you answer that question truthfully, you can truly see the scope of your potential for impact.

- Everything you're doing contributes to your legacy. Achieving time and lifestyle freedom is in service of fulfilling that legacy. When you consider the impact larger than yourself, beyond the financial metrics, you can proceed with purpose.

CONCLUSION

If you've made it this far in the book, congratulations. You are the exact audience I wanted to speak to, and this message is specifically for you. Now that you've reached the peak of this particular mountain, remember it's not the last mountain you'll ever climb. What should you do now, based on the information in each chapter?

You're standing on the peak, and the next step is your choice. You don't have to follow the same path you always have. The next mountain you climb is up to you. Reaching your level of success gives you the security, flexibility, and freedom to choose.

How you climb the mountain—with integrity—is as important as which one you climb. Choose the challenges that fit you best, but use these principles to climb successfully, bring people along with you, and take the experiences and wisdom received from others to guide your way.

You have many new paths and trails to choose from, but your next journey will not be the same as your first mountain climb. You've reached a peak almost no one else reaches and become a different person now. It's time to look at your future from this new elevation and recalibrate your life and your priorities. Once you do that (and by following the steps in this book), you'll achieve the entrepreneurial holy grail: true lifestyle freedom that can only be found *beyond the money*.

P.S. An added bonus for you:

Remember that, when we began this journey, I told you that for his book, I was lucky enough to be able to pick the brains of some of my colleagues and friends I respect the most. You've read some of their perspectives and stories so far. To take that one step further, I will leave you with something special: a brief Q&A with a mentor who has had a most profound impact on me, the top entrepreneur coach in the world, Mr. Dan Sullivan, Co-founder of Strategic Coach®.

⁓

Q: *When was the last time you celebrated a win?*

Dan Sullivan: Probably at about noon today. I would say about three times a day is normal. I have a life filled with wins and celebrations, and I share those with other people.

Q: *How has the demand for your time and attention increased as you've become more successful?*

DS: The demand for my time has increased enormously, but the amount I supply to other people is reduced. I don't open my own mail. I don't answer my own phone. If somebody knocks on our door after 6:00 p.m., we [business and life partner Babs Smith] don't answer. Why should we? It was their idea to knock, not ours.

Q: *What is your thought process when deciding which opportunities to pursue and which to turn down?*

DS: It all goes back to: Does the opportunity support my teamwork with Babs? Does it increase my freedom of time, money, relationships, and purpose? Does it make the Strategic Coach platform stronger? If it doesn't do those things, I don't do that thing. In fact, when people say, "I have an opportunity for you," I often think, "How do you know what I'm looking for opportunity-wise unless you've approached before and tried to learn what I'm looking for? Isn't that part of making it an opportunity for me?"

Q: *Why is it such a challenge for high achievers to give up control?*

DS: It has to do with the fact that they were wired for the first three or four years of their entrepreneurial career that they had to do everything. If they didn't, they could fail. Go bankrupt. And they can't get over the fear and urgency of those early years. My sense is that they mistake control for being in charge. Control means managing things that exist, and being in charge means creating the vision and bringing the energy to inspire others to create the future you envision. Control is about management, and being in charge is about leadership.

Q: *How are you using your time and resources to focus on a purpose you care about or a contribution you'd like to make? Have you thought about your personal legacy?*

DS: My goal in life is to be a coach to the very successful and very driven entrepreneurs so that as they progress, they also become freer. In reality, I am a freedom coach. For me, legacy is only a meaningful term after I die. Thinking in terms of legacy invites death, so I don't think about that. In fact, my greatest wish is that when I die, I'm in the middle of twelve projects. They'll mourn me for a couple of days and then get angry with me because they'll have to contend with my messes. My greatest desire is to lead an incomplete life such that what I leave undone is huge. I have no interest in bringing things to an end.

Q: *Now that having enough money is not really an issue, what are you focusing on? What's important to you and what's next?*

DS: Money has never been an issue for me. It's always been about capability. Money is a useful form of currency that buys capability. If I had to choose between a massive amount of short-term cash and exponential long-term capability, I will take the capability every time.

In fact, I always think of this: Why is it that entrepreneurs take a huge risk early in their lives—their teens or twenties—work very hard, become very successful, and then retire, buying an expensive home in a gated community on a golf course somewhere? In reality, that environment is filled with the kinds of people they became entrepreneurs forty or fifty years before to get away from. They just end up right back there.

It's still got to be about higher growth, higher collaboration, higher creativity. About creating more value. About creating your own happiness and expanding it to other people. And you do that over and over. That's it. That's the secret.

ABOUT THE AUTHOR

Chad Willardson, CFF, CRPC®, AWMA®, is the Founder and President of Pacific Capital, a fiduciary wealth advisory firm he founded in 2011 after nine years of climbing the ranks as an investment advisor at Merrill Lynch. His bestselling first book, *Stress-Free Money*, was featured in *Forbes*'s "21 Books To Read In 2021" and his second book, *Smart, Not Spoiled*, is increasing financial literacy among young people across the country.

In addition to serving the family office clients of Pacific Capital, Chad also manages the $450 million investment portfolio as the elected city treasurer in his community. Chad is recognized as one of the top wealth management experts in the country and has appeared in the *Wall Street Journal*, *Forbes*, *Inc.*, *NBC News*, *Yahoo Finance*, *Nasdaq*, *U.S. News & World Report*, *Investment News*, *Entrepreneur*, and *Financial Advisor* magazine and two bestselling books, *Who Not How* and *The Gap and the Gain* by Dan Sullivan, Dr. Benjamin Hardy, and Tucker Max. He earned his bachelor's degree in economics from Brigham Young University in Provo, Utah. Chad created and trademarked The Financial Life Inspection®, a unique process to remove the stress people feel about their money.

Chad is passionate about financial education and believes that with the right tools and resources, people can be empowered to make smart money decisions. As a Certified Financial Fiduciary®, he loves to help people organize their financial life, clarify their goals, and make decisions that lead them to a successful and fulfilling life. As a father of five, teaching children to be smart and not spoiled is especially important to him. Outside of his business, Chad loves to travel with his family and enjoys playing and watching sports. Chad and his family are very engaged in serving their community. Besides serving as an elected official, he and his family seek out ways to give back to various charitable causes. Chad served as a volunteer for two years on a church service mission in Lithuania, Latvia, Estonia, and Belarus and can speak, read, and write fluently in Lithuanian. Above all, Chad cherishes his family. A native of Orange County, California, Chad and his wife of twenty-one years live in Southern California with their five beautiful children.

CPSIA information can be obtained
at www.ICGtesting.com
Printed in the USA
JSHW011623021222
34075JS00002B/2/J